CW01647177

CRACKING THE CODE ON COMPLEX SENTENCES

The Fastest Way to Jump from Intermediate to Advanced Writing and Get Ahead Academically and Professionally

Since 2000, I have been helping English Language Learners master fundamental writing skills that are rarely covered in the classroom but are essential for academic and professional success:

1. Grammar
2. Essay and report conventions
3. Complex sentences
4. Writing workflows

Complex sentence training has made the greatest difference to my students' writing skills and has had the greatest impact on their communication marks. Moreover, when students know they can write correctly, their confidence in their communication skills rises markedly, and they enjoy school much more.

This training has helped my students excel academically and get into the programs of their choosing. Simply put, mastering academic writing opens big doors.

My publisher wouldn't let me include everything that I wanted to include in this book – he said you'd be overwhelmed! For that reason, your purchase of this book includes:

For that reason, your purchase of this book includes a copy of my new essay writing guides for students:

1. The most powerful, easy-to-use essay structure and content framework on earth will help you craft essays that ANY teacher or professor will love.
2. The pro workflow guide will show you the writing process that professional writers and top students use to consistently get great results on their writing projects.
3. The referencing and plagiarism guide will clarify what plagiarism is, how to avoid it, and how to reference properly.

Together, these three short guides will give you a thorough understanding of the expectations and requirements of academic writing and provide easy-to-understand guidance on how to produce top-quality writing for school.

You can access the guide here (please don't share this link!):
https://aemacademy.ca/complex-sentences-bonuses/

If you are a teacher or homeschooler:

- Access to the course for your school, classes, or children is available for a small fee. Please get in touch: janw@aemacademy.ca

Communication skills are the key to academic and professional success. The world is flooded with workers who have outstanding technical skills. I have seen this repeatedly as a corporate trainer: talented engineers, programmers, and scientists are stuck in technical positions because their managers won't let them communicate directly with clients due to their terrible writing. You simply can't get into leadership roles without exceptional communication skills.

Learning to write well, without grammar mistakes, is the key that unlocks the door to positions of leadership. **Nothing is more important.**

Experience & Qualifications

- **Tutor and instructor**
  - » Since 2000, I've helped over 1000 children, teens, and adults master academic writing.
- **Certified teacher in Ontario**
  - » Since 2011, I've been teaching Grade 12 English, Grade 12 Writer's Craft, Grade 11 English, ESL, and Literacy (OSSLT Preparation).
  - » Online learning coordinator: In 2013, I founded the online learning program at a multinational private high school headquartered in Toronto. During my time there, I developed the "Rolls-Royce" of English training programs, praised by head inspectors from the Ontario Ministry of Education as one of the most effective online language programs they had ever seen. This program helped

hundreds of foreign students get accepted into the most difficult and prestigious university programs in Canada.

- **Certified TESL Ontario ESL teacher**
  - » As a LINC instructor in government-funded programs, I've helped hundreds of newcomers to Canada master business writing, academic writing, and writing for the IELTS exam.
- **Corporate trainer**
  - » As a corporate trainer, I have helped accountants, IT engineers, administrators, scientists, and MBAs improve their speaking and writing skills. Many have been promoted as a direct result of their training.
  - » I have developed custom programs for Chartered Professional Accountants (CPA) of Ontario, Transamerica Life Canada Insurance Company, Financial Services Commission of Ontario, Office of the Fire Marshall of Ontario, and Platform Computing.
- **College and university instructor**
  - » **Henan Agricultural University & Henan University:** Former Business English and ESL instructor; ESL for medical professionals
  - » **Seneca College:** Former essay writing instructor in the academic English preparation program
  - » **University of Ontario Institute of Technology (CultureWorks@ UOIT):** Former essay writing instructor in the academic English preparation program
- **IELTS writing trainer since 2017** (IELTS is a high stakes, high pressure English language exam for university students and professionals)
  - » Former IELTS speaking examiner for IDP Canada
  - » As an IELTS writing trainer, I have been helping students and professionals from around the world get the scores they need on the IELTS examination for PR, medical licensing language requirements, and college and university admission.

Contents

Introduction

This book covers sentence structure in 13 short units, plus a bonus unit on a little-known but profoundly important writing concept: cumulative vs suspensive syntax. You will recognize all these structures because you see them daily. The goal is to draw your attention to them and give you a little bit of practice using them.

The best way to make these lessons stick, though, is to apply what you learn every day in your texts, emails, reports, and essays. You'll see a massive transformation in your writing.

The order of these units is how I build up students' understanding of sentence structure. While the concepts and structures get more complex, the most advanced structures look the simplest and are the shortest, but I can't explain how they work until you understand the earlier, longer structures.

Most people never master writing beyond Level 3. Their writing is full of errors when they attempt constructions at Level 4 and up.

However, learning to write well opens big doors. You can easily master sentence structure and transform the quality of your writing and your quality of life.

Level 1:	Unit 1:	Simple Sentences
	Unit 2:	Compound Sentences
Level 2:	Unit 3:	Passive Voice & Verbs
Level 3:	Unit 4:	Complex Sentences with Subordinate and Relative Clauses (Type I)
	Unit 5:	Conditional Subordinate Clauses
Level 4:	Unit 6:	Semi-Colon Sentences
	Unit 8:	Colon Sentences
Level 5:	Unit 7:	Relative Clauses (Type II-V)
Level 6:	Unit 9:	Participles and Participial Phrases
Level 7:	Unit 10:	Noun Clauses
	Unit 11:	Noun Clauses in Subjunctive Mood
	Unit 12:	Appositives & Adjective Phrases
Level 8:	Unit 13:	Nominative Absolutes
Level 9:	Unit 14:	Cumulative & Suspensive Syntax

1. The Simple Sentence

Key terms

- Adjective
- Adverb
- Complement
- Independent clause
- Noun
- Object
- Predicate
- Preposition
- Subject
- Verb

1.1 Simple Sentence Structures

Let's look at the four most common simple sentence structures. The following fable is written using only these four types of simple sentences.

The Hare and the Tortoise

One day, a hare mocked the tortoise's short legs and slow walk.
The tortoise suggested a race.
The hare was surprised but agreed to race.
On the day of the race, both the hare and the tortoise started at the same time.
The tortoise walked slowly but didn't stop at all.
The hare quickly got far ahead.
In the lead by a mile, he took a nap but slept too long!
The tortoise had already finished the race and was resting.
Slow but steady can win the race.

Subject + Verb + Object

A hare **mocked** a tortoise.
The tortoise **suggested** a race.

At the simplest level, sentences have 2 parts: *a subject* and a predicate, which is the **verb** plus what the verb controls.

The subject is who or what the sentence is about. It's usually a noun: a person, place, thing, or idea.

The predicate is what the subject does to something, what the subject is, or what happens to the subject.

In this case, the predicate includes a **verb** and an object.

An object, like a subject, is a noun.

Subject + Verb + Object is the most basic pattern:

	Subject	**Predicate**	
		Verb	**Object**
1.	A hare	mocked	a tortoise.
2.	The tortoise	suggested	a race.

Subject + Verb + Complement

The hare **was** surprised.

In this case, the **verb** is not an action word. The verb "was" means "=". There's no action in this sentence. The sentence tells us how the hare felt.

"Was" is a variation of the verb "to be." Variations of the verb "to be" include:

- She *is* at home.
- They *were* at work today.
- She *will be* there later.
- He *hasn't been* at school for a month.
- She*'s* upset.
- He *isn't* worried.

In all of these cases, the verb means "equal to" or "not equal to."

After the verb "to be," this predicate has a complement. It's called a "complement" because it "completes" the subject. In other words, it's equivalent to the subject.

Common complements include:

- Nouns
- Adjectives (adjectives modify nouns)
- Preposition phrases (prepositions are the little words that come before places and times).

	Subject	**Predicate**		
		Verb	**Complement**	
1.	The hare	was	a show-off.	**Noun**
2.	The hare	was	surprised.	**Adjective**
3.	The race	was	on Sunday.	**Preposition phrase**

Subject + Verb + Adverb

The tortoise walked slowly.

The hare sprinted ahead.

Adverbs modify verbs.

Adverbs are often formed by adding the suffix *ly* to an adjective.

Adjective: slow	Adjective: silent	Adjective: noisy
Adverb: slowly	Adverb: silently	Adverb: noisily

	Subject	Predicate	
		Verb	Adverb
1.	The tortoise	walked	slowly.
2.	The hare	sprinted	ahead.

Subject + Verb + Preposition phrase

The hare and the tortoise started at the same time.

The tortoise didn't stop on the way.

The hare stopped for a nap.

Prepositions are the little words that indicate where or when something happens.

pre = before
position = place

Literally, a preposition is a word that goes before a place in space or in time: in, on, under, over, before, after, through, for, to, into

	Subject	Predicate	
		Verb	Preposition phrase
1.	The hare and the tortoise	started	at the same time.
2.	The tortoise	didn't stop	on the way.
3.	The hare	stopped	for a nap.

We can add multiple preposition phrases:

	Subject	Predicate		
		Verb	Preposition phrases	
1.	The tortoise	didn't stop	on the way	for any reason.
2.	The hare	stopped	at the park	for a nap.

Simple Sentence = Independent Clause

A subject and predicate combo is called a clause. An independent clause means a subject and predicate combo that makes sense on its own. It's a complete idea by itself.

As we build longer, more complex sentences, we will refer to simple sentences as independent clauses or base clauses to distinguish them from dependent clauses, which are very similar but are not sentences by themselves.

Most of this course will be about the many different types of dependent clauses, as well as other structures called phrases. However, every single sentence MUST have an independent clause as its core.

Remember: No matter how long a sentence is, it MUST have an independent clause. This is the foundation of all sentences.

1.2 Punctuation in Independent Clauses

Punctuation with Preposition Phrases & Adverbs

If the preposition phrase or adverb comes before the independent clause, offset the preposition phrase or adverb with a comma.

- On the way, the tortoise didn't stop for any reason.
- At the park, the hare stopped for a nap.
- Unfortunately, it was too late.

If the preposition phrase or adverb goes after the independent clause, it usually doesn't need a comma.

- The tortoise didn't stop on the way for any reason.
- The hare stopped at the park for a nap.

Proofreading Tip: Always read your work out loud, even if you just mouth the words to yourself. Grammar has a large auditory component – it's the rhythm of the language. Your ears will notice problems that your eyes don't see. For example, commas are used in places where you would naturally pause to help your listener understand. When you read your writing out loud and you find yourself pausing, you probably need punctuation there.

Punctuation with Quoted Speech

If an introductory phrase ends just before the quote begins, use a comma after the phrase and before the opening quotation mark:

- He said**,** "We'll leave at dawn."

If the quote is followed by a tag that states who spoke, use a comma inside the quotation marks before the closing quote (if the quoted expression is not a question or exclamation).

- "It's going to rain**,**" she said.

If the quote is divided into two parts by a tag, use a comma at the end of the first part (inside the quotation marks) and after the tag (unless the tag ends with a question mark or an exclamation point).

- "When we finish dinner**,**" Mom explained**,** "we can watch a movie."

If the quote ends with a question mark or exclamation point, don't add another comma before the closing quotation mark.

- "Are you coming with us**?**" he asked.
- "That's amazing**!**" she exclaimed.

Punctuation with *like* and *such as*

Use a comma before ***like*** or ***such as*** if the information in the *like* phrase is NOT needed for understanding the main idea of the sentence, i.e., the independent clause.

Do not use a comma before ***like*** or ***such as*** if the information in the *like* phrase IS needed for understanding the main idea of the sentence, i.e., the independent clause.

FYI The same punctuation principle applies to:

- Relative clauses (introduced in Unit 4 and covered in depth in Unit 7)
- Appositives (Unit 12)
- Participial phrases (Unit 9).

We'll revisit this issue in those units.

There is NO comma AFTER *such as/like*. This is different from *for example*, which IS followed by a comma.

- A hare caught by an eagle uttered cries like a child.
  - » Without the information after the comma, you would not understand what kind of cries were uttered.
- A peacock said, "I am robed, like a king, in gold and purple and all the colors of the rainbow."
  - » Without the explanation "like a king," you would still know how the peacock looks.

The Oxford Comma

We don't use punctuation when we have two items in a list:

- I want to buy a burger and fries.

When the list contains three or more items, most students are instructed to add a comma between all items except the final one:

- I want to buy a burger, fries and tea.

In the 2nd example, there's no possibility of confusion about what you want. However, in some situations, omitting the comma before the final item can cause confusion:

- For our dinner party, I invited the Smiths, Reggie and Maggie.

In this case, it's not clear how many people were invited for dinner. Is it at least four people (the Smiths plus Reggie and Maggie), or is it two people (Reggie and Maggie being the Smiths)?

This confusion occurs because there's a grammatical structure called an appositive:

- My car, an old Toyota Corolla, is in the shop.
  - » In this case, an old Toyota Corolla = my car.
- The part that I ordered, an X501, has finally arrived.
  - » an X501 = The part that I ordered
- I lent the game to my new friend, Jack.
  - » Jack = new friend

For this reason, to avoid ambiguity, you can add a comma before the final item in a list:

- For our dinner party, I invited the Smiths, Reggie, and Maggie.
  - » Thanks to the final comma, it's now clear that Reggie and Maggie are not the Smiths, so we know at least four people have been invited.

1.2A Punctuation in Independent Clauses

1. This paragraph is missing six periods. Add them.

Canada is a big country in North America it's famous for its friendly people, beautiful landscapes, and cold weather Canada has mountains, forests, lakes, and rivers and is home to many different animals like moose, bears, and beavers in Canada, we speak two official languages: English and French some fun things to do in Canada include ice skating, skiing, going to the beach, camping, and watching hockey if you ever visit Canada, make sure to try poutine, a delicious Canadian dish made of French fries, gravy, and cheese curds

2. This paragraph is missing seven commas. Add them.

Poland is a large country in eastern Europe. It has many beautiful places to visit like sandy beaches by the sea up north and big mountains down south. For outdoor fun you can go hiking in the mountains or kayaking on the lakes. Poland also has many exciting festivals castles and old cities full of stories to discover. The food is good too! In Poland they eat tasty things like dumplings sausages and warm stew with meat and cabbage.

Sentence Fragments

Technically, you can have a one-word sentence, but it has to be a verb, which is the most important word in any sentence. In these cases, the subject is an implied *You*:

- Stop!
- Go!

For the most part, however, a sentence is composed of a **subject** and a <u>predicate</u>, which is at least a *verb*. Together, a subject + predicate combo is called an independent clause.

- **He** <u>*loves* noodles</u>.
- **He** <u>*eats* noisily</u>.
- **He** <u>*eats* at his desk</u>.

If you don't have both a subject and a predicate, you've usually only got part of a sentence, which we call a fragment.

1. In the morning.
    - There's no subject or verb, so this is not an independent clause. It's a preposition phrase.
2. Works too hard.
    - There's no subject, so this is not an independent clause. It's a predicate.
3. Everything wrong.
    - There's no verb. It's not an independent clause.

1.2B Independent Clause or Fragment?

Are these proper independent clauses or fragments?

a)	Independent clause	Fragment	When a student is given a math test or a question.
b)	Independent clause	Fragment	The main cause of drunk driving.
c)	Independent clause	Fragment	I prefer staying at home.
d)	Independent clause	Fragment	Firstly, there is expertise.
e)	Independent clause	Fragment	People with a healthy lifestyle generally feel good about themselves.
f)	Independent clause	Fragment	If you have high blood pressure for an extended period of time.
g)	Independent clause	Fragment	First, the causes of waste in the ocean.
h)	Independent clause	Fragment	Is one of the richest and most popular YouTubers.
i)	Independent clause	Fragment	For example, a backpack and a hat.
j)	Independent clause	Fragment	It's over.

1.2C Review of Key Concepts in Simple Sentences

1. What is the technical term for a simple sentence? ______________________

2. What is a clause? A clause typically consists of a/an____________followed by a/an_________, which is made up of at least a/an _________ and the words after it. A subject is generally a/an ____________ . So is an object.

The Dog and His Reflection

A dog had stolen a piece of meat out of a butcher's shop.

On his way home, he was crossing a river.

He saw his reflection in the stream below.

He mistook it for another dog with another piece of meat.

Greedily, he resolved to secure the meat.

He snapped at his supposed treasure.

Unfortunately, he dropped his piece of meat and so lost all.

3. Identify the SUBJECT in each sentence.

a) A dog had stolen a piece of meat out of a butcher's shop.

b) On his way home, he was crossing a river.

4. Identify the complete VERB in each sentence.

a) A dog had stolen a piece of meat out of a butcher's shop.

b) On his way home, he was crossing a river.

c) He saw his reflection in the stream below.

d) He dropped his piece of meat and so lost all.

5. Identify the PREDICATE in each sentence.

a) On his way home, he was crossing a river.

b) He saw his reflection in the stream below.

6. Identify the complete OBJECT in each sentence.

a) A dog had stolen a piece of meat out of a butcher's shop.

b) Hewas crossing a river.

c) He saw his reflection in the stream below.

d) Unfortunately, he dropped his piece of meat and so lost all.

7. Identify the ADVERB in each sentence.

a) Greedily, he resolved to secure the meat.

b) Unfortunately, he dropped his piece of meat and so lost all.

8. Identify the PREPOSITION/S in each sentence.

a) A dog had stolen a piece of meat out of a butcher's shop.

b) On his way home, he was crossing a river.

c) He mistook it for another dog with another piece of meat.

9. This fable is missing eight periods. Write them in.

The Crow and the Pitcher

A crow was nearly dead from thirst he spied a pitcher with a little water in it unfortunately, the level of water was very low he strained to sip the water but couldn't reach it with his beak then he tried to overturn and break the pitcher he was not strong enough for that at last, he spotted some small pebbles and dropped them one by one into the pitcher in this way, he raised the water to the brim and quenched his thirst

10. This fable is missing five commas. Write them in.

The Fox and the Lion

For the very first time a young fox saw a lion and was ready to die of fear. The second time he took courage and could even bear to look upon him. The third time he came up to him saluted him and had a conversation with him.

11. Analyze the structure of each sentence and label its parts. Many labels will be needed more than once.

adverb	preposition phrase
complement	subject
object	verb

Labels					
a)	A crow	was	nearly dead	from thirst.	
Labels					
b)	He	spied	a pitcher	with a little water	in it.
Labels					
c)	Unfortunately,	the level of water	was	very low.	
Labels					
d)	He	spotted	some small pebbles.		

1.3 Simple Sentences with Dummy Subjects

Dummy Subject #1: It Is

You'll often see sentences beginning with *It is*. In these examples, *it is* or *it's* has no meaning:

- **It's** a pleasure to meet you.
- **It's** not possible to do that. **It isn't** possible to do that.
- **It's not** fair that he gets to go and I don't.

Dummy Subject #2: There Is

You'll often see sentences beginning with *There is*. In these examples, *there is/ there are* has no meaning – it just means that something exists/doesn't exist:

- **There are** only a few people in line ahead of you.
- **There aren't** any tickets left.
- **There isn't** enough time to do it.
- **There's** been an accident.

In many cases, such sentences can be rewritten to eliminate the dummy subject. Which version sounds better?

There are only a few people in line ahead of you.	Only a few people are in line ahead of you.
There aren't any tickets left.	No tickets are left.
There isn't enough time to do it.	We don't have time to do it.
There's been an accident.	An accident has occurred.

1.3A Review

Transform these sentences to remove the dummy subject constructions. There are many ways to do this.

1. There's nothing in the world like ice cream.

2. There is no believing a liar, even when he speaks the truth.

3. To get what I want, there is nothing that I wouldn't promise.

4. There is a bone stuck in my throat.

5. There are many treasures hidden in the cave.

6. There aren't enough snacks to go around.

7. There are no clouds in sight.

8. There are many footprints going into the lion's den, but there are none coming out.

9. It is shocking how badly she behaves.

10. It isn't kind to say such things!

11. It is safer to be among friends than enemies.

12. It's impossible to finish this on time.

1.4 Parallelism in Lists

In a list, every item needs to have the same grammatical structure. This structure is controlled by the first item in the list. Every item after the first item needs to be consistent in grammatical structure.

I love <u>drawing, to cook with my mom, and read books</u>.

- In this case, <u>all three items in the list</u> have different grammatical constructions:
  - » drawing
  - » to cook
  - » read

- All three items need to have the same grammatical form. Solutions:
  - » I love drawing, cooking with my mom, and reading books.
  - » I love to draw, cook with my mom, and read books.

1.4A Parallel Structure in Lists - Fix the Errors (Level 1)

Instructions: Fix the parallelism error in each sentence.

1. She enjoys hiking, jogging, and to swim in the lake.

____

____

2. He wants to improve his cooking skills, learning to make sushi, and to create his own pasta dishes.

____

____

3. She wants to learn Spanish, to travel to Mexico, and just relaxing on the beach.

____

____

4. To become a successful musician, you must have talent, dedicated, practice regularly, and to study music theory.

____

____

5. There are several solutions to pollution: cleaning up garbage, don't drive if you don't need to, and to use products that are not toxic for the environment.

____

____

6. Job search websites make it is easy to search for work, uploading documents, and communication with potential employers.

____

____

7. Robots do things more quickly than people, like calculate large numbers, cracking codes, and performance of actions repeatedly and accurately.

____

____

8. There are three major benefits of learning another language: enjoy foreign films, communication without barriers, and being able to work or study overseas.

____

____

9. Victims of the disease can go insane, fall into a coma, and possibly even death

____

____

1.4B Parallel Structure in Lists - Fix the Errors (Level 2)

Instructions: Fix the parallelism error in each sentence.

1. In conclusion, pollution can harm our health, dying creatures, and it can poison the soil.

____

____

2. If you want to become a nurse, you need positive qualities such as being hardworking, caring, patience and confidence.

___

___

3. As resources are consumed, forest habitats will be destroyed, species killed off, and disturbing indigenous people.

___

___

4. On my mom's smartphone, we can learn what the weather will be, watching our favorite shows and news, or even gaming.

___

___

5. Children are constantly watching how their parents juggle work, pay the bills, and investing.

___

___

6. Workplace harassment can make people feel stressed, poor performance, and wanting to quit their job.

___

___

7. Cyberbullying can cause some teenagers to drop out socially, isolating themselves, and their grades drop.

____

____

8. In summary, there are major differences in communication, our lifestyle, and study before and after the internet.

____

____

9. The ideal job candidate must have excellent communication skills, experienced in marketing, and able to work under pressure.

____

____

1.5 Pronoun Referencing

- **Antecedent**: the specific noun that a pronoun refers back to

Pronouns replace nouns. If you're talking about John, you're not going to keep repeating "John did A... John did B.... John did C." You're going to switch to *He* after the first *John*.

A pronoun MUST match the specific noun it's replacing. Otherwise, the audience is confused about what the pronoun *refers* to – that's why this issue is called pronoun *referencing*.

This is a cohesion (sticking together) problem: it's not clear how ideas are connected to each other if pronouns don't match their antecedents. For example, if I'm talking about *computers* and then switch to *it*, the audience will be confused because *computers* is plural but *it* is singular. Conversely, if I'm talking about *a computer*, it would be confusing to switch to *they*.

Cohesion Tip: In general, avoid pronouns in paragraph topic sentences. Using a pronoun in a topic sentence forces the reader to try to figure out what the pronoun matches in a preceding paragraph. Keep nouns in topic sentences specific.

1.5A Pronoun Referencing - Fix the Errors (Level 1)

Instructions: Fix the pronoun referencing error in each sentence.

1. The telephone is one of the most important inventions of all time. First, it plays a crucial role in emergency situations. For instance, they allow people to quickly contact emergency services, such as police, the fire department, or medical professionals.
2. Humanoid robots will soon be able to perform complex tasks on its own.
3. Once you finish sautéing the vegetables, put it in the tortilla.
4. Job websites are the best solution for job seekers because it lists more jobs than any newspaper.
5. Some movies are good because it is funny, and we can learn a lot about life.
6. In this game, we collect gems and coins to unlock powers in your avatar.
7. In the game, if you're not fast enough collecting coins, someone else will take it and you have to restart the level.
8. You watch one tutorial video after another and work on the problems until you are able to solve it.
9. Dogs serve different purposes to its owners.
10. Some dogs are aggressive and probably wouldn't be great with kids, unless it is well trained.

1.5B Pronoun Referencing - Fix the Errors (Level 2)

Instructions: Fix the pronoun referencing error/s in each sentence. At the end of each question, the number in parentheses indicates the number of errors in that sentence.

1. Close friends are someone you can share your hopes and dreams with. (1)
2. The problem with books is that they take up a lot of time. People can easily spend hours in your bedroom reading books. (1)
3. Smartphones have had an enormous effect on our daily lives. It has given nearly all humans the ability to talk to other people anywhere in the world. (1)
4. It's not a good idea to keep exotic pets. For example, a baby tiger might be manageable, but when a tiger grows up, they can effortlessly kill their owners. (2)
5. Fake friends don't really like you. They might be friendly at first, but later she will try to take something from you. (1)
6. Laptop computers are very portable as they are compact. You can easily fit it in your backpack, or you can store it in your desk.(2)
7. People spend an unreasonable amount of time on our phones alone in our rooms. (2)
8. The sun pulls the planets to it, so it does not drift away. (2)
9. Take two slices of whole wheat bread and toast it for three minutes. Next, get your onion and cut them into small strips.(2)
10. Effluent from factories poisons the water. They kill a lot of marine life. (1)
11. Computers can help children with their education. Some apps, such as Word and Notes, allow you to type your assignments.Others, such as Duolingo, IXL, and Grammarly, help you get ahead at school.(3)

2. Compound Sentences

2.1 Coordinating conjunctions

Coordinating conjunctions are the most common joining words: but, and, nor, so, or, yet, for.

The easiest way to lengthen your sentences is to join two simple sentences (independent clauses) together with a coordinating conjunction.

Independent clause	Comma	Coordinating conjunction	Independent clause
My dog is wet	,	**so**	he really smells.
My teacher isn't too smart	,	**but**	she's an easy marker.
We can order pizza	,	**or**	I can make peanut butter sandwiches.

Conjunctions are joining words. There are 4 types of conjunctions, but the focus of this unit is on the 1st type, coordinating conjunctions. They are the simplest and most common joining words, and you can remember them by the acronym **BAN SOY**:

- **b**ut
- **a**nd
- **n**or
- **s**o
- **o**r
- **y**et
- Many texts list ***for*** as a coordinating conjunction, but it has become archaic (old-fashioned) and hardly ever used. If you do see *for* being used as a conjunction, it means *because*.

Compound Sentences with *Nor*

In compound sentences joined using *nor*, the second sentence inverts the order of subject + auxiliary verb (helper verb) + negative, and *not* becomes *nor*:

I couldn't find all the spices. **I couldn't** get the fresh herbs.

- I could<u>n't</u> > <u>nor</u> could I

I couldn't find all the spices, **nor could I** get the fresh herbs.

She wasn't available on Monday. **She's not** available today.

- She's <u>not</u> > <u>nor</u> is she

She wasn't available on Monday, **nor is she** available today.

Punctuation in Compound Sentences

In general, use a comma BEFORE the coordinating conjunction. However, if both independent clauses are short, many authors will not use a comma. That being said, most teachers expect a comma, so it's safer to use one for a school assignment. In the examples below, I've used a comma in some and no comma in the others. Read them out loud: do you find that a pause is necessary before the conjunction? If so, use a comma.

Note: Both sides of the coordinating conjunction MUST BE independent clauses, i.e., stand-alone sentences.

- I love pizza, **but** I shouldn't eat too much.
- I cooked the soup **and** my mom baked the bread.
- I couldn't find all the spices, **nor** could I get the fresh herbs.
- I prepared the ingredients early **so** I can cook right away.
- We can eat out, **or** we can cook at home.
- I followed the instructions, **yet** it doesn't taste right.

Then Is Not a Coordinating Conjunction

Then is NOT a coordinating conjunction. Using *then* as a coordinating conjunction results in a run-on sentence (ROS). The simple solution is to use *and then* in the middle of a sentence.

INCORRECT	Yesterday, I went to school, then I went to the park.
	This is an ROS (run-on sentence).
CORRECT	Yesterday, I went to school, and then I went to the park.
ALSO CORRECT	Yesterday, I went to school; then, I went to the park.
	We will cover this last format in Unit 6: Semi-colon + Conjunctive Adverb Sentences. Very briefly, *then* is a conjunctive adverb like *however* and *therefore*. You can use a conjunctive adverb followed by a comma at the beginning of a sentence, but you can also use a semi-colon + conjunctive adverb + comma combo to join two independent clauses, as in the last example above.

Can You Start a Sentence with a Coordinating Conjunction?

Yes, you can. There is no rule against starting a sentence with a coordinating conjunction. However, don't do it more than once or twice per page, or once in a short response. Due to the brevity of coordinating conjunctions – they're all 2 and 3 letter words – their effect is abrupt and thus noticeable: starting too many sentences with coordinating conjunctions gives your writing a breathless feeling. So use them sparingly (like in this sentence).

Run-on Sentences (ROS)

If you have two independent clauses, you cannot separate them with a comma (or nothing at all between them):

I love pizza, ROS I shouldn't eat too much.

Both *I love pizza* and *I shouldn't eat too much* are perfectly good simple sentences, i.e., independent clauses. We're not allowed to separate them with just a comma. We need to use a period or a coordinating conjunction (BAN SOY: but, and, nor, so, or, yet).

We can also transform one of the clauses into a dependent clause in order to make a complex sentence, or we can use a semi-colon, which functions very much like a period. These options will appear below, but you should consult those sections of this course for an explanation of how to use these more advanced constructions.

I love pizza, ROS **I shouldn't eat too much.**

Solution 1: Use a period.	I love pizza. I shouldn't eat too much.
Solution 2: Use a coordinating conjunction.	I love pizza**, but** I shouldn't eat too much.
Solution 3: Transform one of the independent clauses into a dependent clause, which gives you a complex sentence (covered in Unit 4).	**Although** I love pizza, I shouldn't eat too much. I love pizza **although** I shouldn't eat too much.
Solution 4: Use a semi-colon + conjunctive adverb + comma combo.	I love pizza**; however,** I shouldn't eat too much.

2.1A Coordinating Conjunctions – Use the Correct Coordinating Conjunction to Improve This Fable

Add appropriate coordinating conjunctions to this fable.

The Wolf and the Lamb

A wolf and a lamb came to a brook to quench their thirst.

The wolf stood high up the stream, 1) __________ the lamb stood a little distance below.

The wolf made up his mind to seize the lamb, 2) __________ he thought about how to justify his act of violence. He roared, "How dare you muddy the water 3) __________ I cannot drink it?"

The lamb was taken aback by the accusation. She humbly responded, "the water runs down from you to me, 4) __________ how could I possibly muddy it?"

The wolf retorted, "be that as it may, 5) __________ you are still a rascal. You said bad things about me last year behind my back."

The lamb replied, "That's impossible! A year ago, I wasn't born, 6) __________ that couldn't have been me."

"It's all the same," growled the wolf, 7) __________ he jumped upon the lamb and tore her to pieces."

2.1B Coordinating Conjunctions – Use the Correct Coordinating Conjunction to Improve This Fable

Add appropriate coordinating conjunctions to this fable.

The Man and His Two Sweethearts

A middle-aged man with graying hair courted two women at the same time.

One of them was young, 1) __________ the other was well-advanced in years.

The older woman was ashamed to be courted by a younger man, 2) __________ she made a point of pulling out some of his black hairs.

The younger, on the contrary, did not wish to become the wife of an old man, 3) __________ she was equally zealous in removing his gray hair.

Between the two of them, he very soon lost every hair left on his head.

Try to please everybody 4) __________ you will please nobody.

2.2 Correlative Conjunctions

Correlative conjunctions are pairs of words that work together to join words, phrases, or clauses in a sentence and show the relationship between the elements they are connecting.

These pairs are used to link similar grammatical elements (like nouns to nouns, verbs to verbs, or clauses to clauses) and they can lend a sense of balance and rhythm to sentences.

Common correlative conjunction pairs:

1. **either...or:** Used to present two alternatives.
   » You can either study hard or relax during the holidays.
2. **neither...nor:** Used to negate both parts of a statement.
   » She is neither going to the party nor staying home.
3. **both...and:** Used to emphasize the link between two items.
   » Both the movie and the book were excellent.
4. **not only...but also:** Used to add emphasis to an additional element.
   » She is not only intelligent but also very kind.
5. **whether...or:** Used to present two possibilities, often when there's a choice or doubt.
   » I don't know whether to buy the red dress or the blue one.
6. **as...as:** Used to make comparisons showing equality.
   » He is as tall as his brother.
7. **such...that:** Used to indicate cause and effect.
   » It was such a sunny day that we went to the beach.
8. **no sooner...than:** Used to show that one thing happens immediately after another.
   » No sooner had I arrived home than the phone rang.
9. **rather...than:** Used to express a preference.
   » I would rather go hiking than stay indoors.
10. **not...but:** Used to correct or clarify a previous statement.
    » I am not angry but disappointed.

11. **just as ... so (too)**:
    » Just as your great grandfather was a farmer, so too was your grandfather.

2.2A Use a correlative conjunction pair to complete each sentence

as...as...	neither...nor...	rather...than...
both...and...	no sooner...than...	such...that...
either...or...	not only...but also...	whether...or...
just as...so...	not...but (rather)...\	

1. __________ had she started to read the book __________ she realized she had read it before.
2. __________ the teacher __________ the students were eager to start the project.
3. __________ water is essential for plants, __________ is sunlight necessary for their growth.
4. I can't decide __________ to bake a cake __________ make cookies for the dessert.
5. I would __________ cook at home __________ risk food poisoning.
6. She was __________ upset, __________ rather surprised by the news.
7. The concert was __________ a success __________ they are planning a second show.
8. The movie was __________ exciting __________ interesting.
9. The museum is __________ a place of history __________ a center for community events.
10. The puppy is __________ playful __________ it is adorable.
11. You must __________ finish your homework __________ help with the chores.

3. The Verb System & Passive Constructions

The verb is the most important word in a sentence. In fact, if you don't have a verb, you don't have a sentence. The verb is so important because it is the lynchpin that connects the subject (who or what the sentence is about) with the predicate (what the subject is, what the subject does/has, what happens to the subject).

The verb changes its form based on context. We modify the form of a verb (this is called conjugation) based on 4 factors:

1. **Time:** 12 verb times (often called "tenses")
2. **Person & number:** 6 possible subject types
3. **Voice:** active & passive constructions
4. **Mood:** suggestions & orders require subjunctive mood (covered in section 11. Noun Clauses in Subjunctive Mood)

Time, person & number, and voice are covered in **3.1 Present Verbs** below.

1. We modify verbs based on TIME.

There are 12 ways to express time (usually called verb "tenses"):

Past

Past simple Past action that's finished	The wolf **caught** a lamb.
Past continuous Interrupted action: past continuous is used for the ongoing action; past simple is used for the interruption	While the wolf **was eating** the lamb, a lion stole it from him.
Past perfect Past action that occurred at some point before another past action	The lion **hadn't eaten** anything in several days, so he was famished.
Past perfect continuous Past action that occurred right before another past action	The lion **had been hunting** for nearly a week before he came upon the wolf.

3.0A Use the correct past forms of the verbs in this fable

You'll need to use each of the four forms at least once.

The Fisherman and the Little Fish

A fisherman **1) (toil)** ______________________ all day and **2) (catch)** ______________________ nothing, but as he was about to leave, he **3) (pull up)** ______________________ a little fish. While he **4) (reel)** ______________________ it in, the fish **5) (beg)** ______________________ him to let him go. He was small now, he said, but by and by, he would grow to be a big fish and so he would be worth catching. The fisherman **6) (answer)** ______________________, "No, I have you now, but I might not get you later, so it would be foolish of me to let you go."

A fish in the hand is worth two in the lake.

Present

Present simple Facts, actions that regularly occur	The birds **wake** me up every day with their song.
Present continuous An action occurring right now	The birds **are chirping** outside the window.
Present perfect Experience, current significance of a past event	I **have never heard** such a beautiful sound.
Present perfect continuous An action that started in the past and is still occurring	They've **been singing** all morning.

3.0B Use the correct present forms of the verbs in this fable

You'll need to use each of the four forms at least once.

The Hare

Predators like dogs **1) (chase)** _____________________ hares constantly. To outwit them, hares **2) (possess)** _____________________ a good deal of cunning. Du Fouilloux, a French naturalist, **3) (report)** _____________________ many interesting facts about hares:

- To escape dogs, hares **4) (join)** _____________________ a flock of sheep in the field and stayed at their feet.
- Hares **5) (hide)** _____________________ themselves among the rushes near a pond.
- Hares **6) (mount)** _____________________ six-foot-high walls.
- When dogs **7) (chase)** _____________________ a hare for hours, the hare **8) (trade)** _____________________ places with another hare.

Future

Note 1: Present continuous is most commonly used for future situations.

- We**'re going** to the park this weekend.

Note 2: Future perfect and future perfect continuous are rarely used.

Future simple Intentions about the future	I **will look** for a new job next year.
Future continuous Ongoing action in the future; often used for predictions	I **will be working** at my current job while I look for another one.
Future perfect Experience from a future perspective	Until now, I have worked at 3 schools. If I get another teaching job, I **will have worked** at 4 different schools.
Future perfect continuous Describing something that starts BEFORE a future point in time AND will also be ongoing at that future point in time	I've been working at my current job for 9 years. If I stay here, by next year, I **will have been working** here for 10 years.

3.0C Use the correct future forms of the verbs in this career advice for young people

You'll need to use each of the four forms at least once.

Preparing for a Career

- Exploring different hobbies and interests **1) (help)** ______________________ you find your true calling.
- Over the next year, you **2) (learn)** ______________________ many new subjects in school.
- By the time you finish your education, you **3) (gain)** ______________________ a variety of skills that employers will find valuable.
- By the time you start your first job, you **4) (prepare)** ______________________ for it for many years through your education, hobbies, and any part-time jobs.
- You **5) (meet)** ______________________ many people throughout your education and early career.
- During career studies at school, you **6) (explore)** __________________ various career options. You **7) (shape)** ______________________ your understanding of different fields, so always ask questions and seek advice from teachers and professionals.
- By the time you are considering your first major career move, you **8) (explore)** ______________________ different interests and developing skills for many years.

2. We modify verbs based on PERSON and NUMBER.

The most common mistake is omitting the s at the end of present simple verbs with a 3rd person singular subject:

Subject			Predicate	
Person	**Number**		**Verb**	**Object**
1st person	**singular**	I	love	pizza.
2nd person	**singular**	You	love	pizza.
3rd person	**singular**	She/He	love**s**	pizza.
1st person	**plural**	We	love	pizza.
2nd person	**plural**	You	love	pizza.
3rd person	**plural**	They	love	pizza.

3. We also modify verbs based on VOICE.

The voice of the verb (also known as the agent of the verb) can precede the verb, follow the verb, or be omitted:

1. The crowd always **boos** this referee.
   - » The voice of the booing precedes the **verb**.
2. The referee **is being booed** by the crowd.
   - » The voice of the booing follows the **verb**.
3. The referee **is being booed** *constantly for his bad calls.*
   - » It's obvious that a crowd is doing the booing, so this voice information has been omitted. The focus of this sentence is on *the frequency* and *the reason*.

The simplest way to think about passive voice is that the subject and object of the **verb** are trading places. However, this results in confusing terminology, so we refer to the noun that controls the verb as the agent, and we refer to the noun that is being controlled as the *patient*. This way, the terminology remains consistent:

- Active voice: The baker **is baking** *the cake*.
- Passive voice: *The cake* **is being baked** by the baker.

The baker does the baking, so the baker is the agent of the verb in both the active and passive form. The cake does NOT do the baking, so the cake is the *patient* of the verb in both the active and passive form.

Sentence Structure Flip

Using passive voice lets you flip the subject and object in a sentence. This can be useful for making a sentence better match the preceding and following sentences. An important principle of cohesion (how ideas stick together) is that the end of a sentence should match the beginning of the next sentence. Switching between active and passive voice is a good strategy to flip the order of sentence elements.

We'll now look at the 4 present verbs. Keep in mind that the names of the verbs are the same in past, present, and future (3X simple, continuous, perfect, and perfect continuous).

Present Verbs

3.1A Present Simple

Present simple, the most commonly used verb tense, is for general facts, daily routines, and beliefs, i.e. for things that are always/generally true. In these cases, time doesn't matter:

- The sun **rises** in the east and **sets** in the west.
- I **enjoy** walks on the beach.
- My cat **doesn't like** her.

Conjugation for Person & Number

The first type of modification we'll talk about is **conjugation for person and number**. We change the ending of the verb depending on the subject. Be careful with the ending on 3rd person singular:

SUBJECT		**PREDICATE**	
Person & number		**Verb**	**Rest of predicate**
1st person singular	I	wake up	at 5 AM.
2nd person singular	You	wake up	at 5 AM.
3rd person singular	He/she/it	wake**s** up	at 5 AM.
1st person plural	We	wake up	at 5 AM.
2nd person plural	You	wake up	at 5 AM.
3rd person plural	They	wake up	at 5 AM.

Common Mistake #1: Subject-Verb Agreement for 3rd Person Singular Verbs

By far, the most common mistake in English grammar is subject-verb agreement (SVA) for third person singular (he, she, it). The grammar rule is completely illogical. You just have to remember it:

- I love pizza.
- You love pizza.
- He/She loves pizza.
- We love pizza.
- They love pizza.

Common Mistake #2: Subject-Verb Agreement (SVA) with Long Subjects Containing Both Singular and Plural Words

Sometimes, long subjects have both singular and plural words. With long subjects, look at the first noun/noun phrase of the full subject and decide whether it's a singular or plural idea.

In the two examples below, <u>the complete subject</u> is underlined. The **noun/noun phrase** at the beginning is **bolded**:

1. <u>Practical subjects such as automotive repair and culinary arts</u> **BENEFIT** students more than humanities subjects.
    1. **Practical subjects** is plural.
2. <u>Taking practical subjects such as automotive repair and culinary arts</u> **BENEFITS** students more than taking humanities subjects.
    1. **Taking** is singular.

3.1A Are these situations singular or plural? Use the correct form of the verb

1. Compared to life in developed countries, life in developing countries **is/are** much more difficult.
2. Studies have shown that daily screen time for children ages 9 and up **has/have** been increasing.
3. The age group that is most likely to get cyberbullied on social media **is/are** teenagers that are female (DoSomething and Pew Research Center).
4. Using cell phones **is/are** disrespectful and disruptive in meetings.
5. The transportation of milk containers **is/are** done by milk tanker daily.
6. The increasing number of security cameras that are installed in private and government premises **has/have** brought down crime rates of robberies and thefts significantly.
7. The number of infected patients **is/are** under control.
8. The use of devices such as cell phones, GPS watches, and trackers **has/have** been gaining popularity for obvious reasons.
9. In conclusion, the benefits of the technologies for monitoring and tracking people clearly **exceed/exceeds** the disadvantages.

Conjugation for Active/Passive Voice

Voice refers to the orientation of the subject and object around the verb. This has nothing to do with verb tense/time.

Active voice is the default subject-*verb*-<u>object</u> orientation:	The bakers *bake* <u>the bread</u> at 5 AM.
Passive voice is when we move the object in front of the *verb*:	The bread *is baked* by the bakers at 5 AM.
Passive voice also allows us to remove information about who or what is responsible for the action:	The bread is baked at 5 AM. We can omit "by the bakers" if we think it's too obvious.

Passive voice is when we take the object and place it in front of the verb. We can move the subject after the verb, or we can leave it out. Why? In some cases, keeping the subject produces a baby English sentence, like the example above. Who bakes bread? Only bakers bake bread, so it isn't necessary to say so. In this case, passive voice would make a better sentence.

We use the concepts *agent of the verb* & *patient of the verb* to clarify this:

- The **agent of the verb** is the noun that is responsible for controlling the verb.
- The **patient of the verb** is the noun that is controlled by the verb, like a patient is controlled by doctors/nurses while in their care.
- Note: BOTH examples are in present simple (not past tense).

The bakers	**bake**	**the bread**	**at 5 AM.**
AGENT of the verb	VERB: present simple, active voice	PATIENT of the verb	Preposition phrase

The bread	**is baked**	**(by the bakers)**	**at 5 AM.**
PATIENT of the verb	VERB: present simple, passive voice	AGENT of the verb (not needed in this case since it's obvious)	Preposition phrase

	Passive Voice	**Active Voice**
1st person singular	I **am picked up** at the corner at 8 AM.	The bus **picks** me **up** at the corner at 8 AM.
2nd person singular	You **are picked up** at home at 8:15 AM.	The bus **picks** you **up** at home at 8:15 AM.
3rd person singular	Lisa **is not picked up** until 8:30 AM. This new policy **is believed to be** a good idea. **It is believed** that this new policy is a good idea. • This dummy subject construction is commonly used for passive voice.	The bus **does not pick up** Lisa until 8:30 AM. Some people **believe** this new policy **is** a good idea.
1st person plural	We **aren't liked** by anybody.	Nobody **likes** us.

	Passive Voice	Active Voice
2nd person plural	You **are driven** to school because it's too far to walk.	My dad **drives** us to school because it's too far to walk.
3rd person plural	Those older students **are** not **driven** to school because they have their own car.	Nobody **drives** those older students to school because they have their own car.

Transform these sentences into their passive forms:

Note: You might need to include an adverb between the auxiliary and the main verb.

	Passive Voice	Active Voice
1st person singular	I _______________ to the annual gala every year.	The committee **invites** me to the annual gala every year.
2nd person singular	Every year, you _______________ for your athletic achievements.	Every year, the school **recognizes** you for your athletic achievements.
3rd person singular	She _______________ at home alone while her parents travel.	Her parents **often leave** her at home alone while they travel.
1st person plural	We _______________ about policy changes at the last second.	The authorities **only inform** us about policy changes at the last second.
2nd person plural	You all _______________ for your volunteer work.	The organization **appreciates** you all for your volunteer work.
3rd person plural	They _______________ experts in their field.	Many **consider** them experts in their field.

3.2 Present Continuous

Present continuous describes what's happening *right now.* It's also commonly used to describe future intentions.

- I'**m coming** to get you *right now.*
- Stop it! You'**re being** unreasonable.
- You guys sound like you'**re getting** sick.
- We'**re going** camping next month.

	Passive Voice	Active Voice
1st person singular	Help! I'**m being chased** by a bear.	Help! A bear **is chasing** me.
2nd person singular or plural	You'**re being treated** very unfairly.	The teacher **is treating** you very unfairly.
3rd person singular	She **is being seen** right now.	We **are seeing** her *right now.*
1st person plural	We'**re being given** a huge discount.	They'**re giving** us a huge discount.
3rd person plural	The broken parts **are being fixed** *at the moment.*	They **are fixing** the broken parts *at the moment.*

3.2A Transform these sentences into their passive forms:

Note: You might need to include an adverb between the auxiliary and the main verb.

	Passive Voice	Active Voice
1st person singular	I ______________________________ my own department to run.	The company **is giving** me my own department to run.
2nd person singular or plural	You ____________________ a raise next month!	The company **is giving** you a raise next month!
3rd person singular	Dinner _______________________ at the moment.	He'**s cooking** dinner at the moment.
1st person plural	We ___________________________ ______ next month.	The company **is probably laying** us **off** next month.
3rd person plural	New patients _________________ ______________________________.	The doctor **is now accepting** new patients.

3.3 Present Perfect

Present perfect describes experiences and the results of actions that started in the past. Even though they happened in the past, they are relevant now.

- **Have** you ever **seen** Batman? Yes, I **have seen** it.
- **Have** you **eaten**? No, I **have**n't_**eaten** yet.
- **Have** you ever **tried** perogies? Yes, I'**ve had** them many times.

- Which countries **have** you **visited**? I**'ve visited** China, Poland, and France.

The present perfect answer indicates that you have experienced being in these countries. Present perfect does not provide any specific information about when those experiences occurred in the past. In this example, the speaker is not indicating when he visited China, Poland, and France; he is not even indicating that he visited those countries in that order.

- **Have** you **heard** the news? No, I **have**n't **heard** anything.
- He still **hasn't recovered** from the accident.
- The policy **hasn't resulted** in any improvements.

	Passive Voice	**Active Voice**
1st person singular	I **haven't been given** a form to fill out.	No one **has given** me a form to fill out.
2nd person singular or plural	**Have** you **been seen** by anyone?	**Has** anyone **seen** you?
3rd person singular	Has she **been given** the medicine?	**Has** anyone **given** her the medicine?
1st person plural	No, we **haven't been seen** by anyone yet.	No, no one **has seen** us yet.
3rd person plural	They **haven't been given** an explanation	Nobody has given them an explanation.

Note 1: In passive voice, *been* is pronounced *bin.*

Note 2: The verb *have* is not used passively.

Active voice: I**'ve** always **had** these migraines.

Passive voice: These migraines ~~have always been had by me~~. Yuk!

In movies, especially older American crime dramas, you'll hear the expression "We've been had!" It means "We've been cheated." This expression is not commonly used today.

3.3A Transform these sentences into their passive forms:

Note: You might need to include an adverb between the auxiliary and the main verb.

	Passive Voice	Active Voice
1st person singular	I ________________________________by many people along the way.	Many people **have helped** me along the way.
2nd person singular or plural	You ______________________________ bad information.	Somebody **has given** you bad information.
3rd person singular	_______ she __________________________?	**Has** anyone **seen** her?
1st person plural	We ___________________ when we _____ ______________________________.	They **haven't told** us when they **will see** us.
3rd person plural	They ___________________ to leave or the police _________________________.	The staff **have told** them to leave or they **will call** the police.

Present Perfect vs Past Simple

Present perfect is about the present significance of something that happened in the past or that started in the past:

- Have you ever seen/visited/heard...?
- Have you ever broken a bone?
- Have you eaten? = Are you hungry now?

Past simple asks specific questions about events that ended in the past.

- Did you watch the news last night?
- When did you break your leg?
- What did you eat for lunch?

Questions in past simple often follow present perfect questions:

Present perfect asks whether the experience occurred.	Q. Have you ever lived overseas? A. Yes, I have lived overseas.
Past simple asks and answers about specific past events.	Q. Where did you live? A. I lived in China for a couple years.

Statements using past simple mean that the action happened in the past. Statements using present perfect mean that the action happened in the past, and its consequences are significant now:

Present perfect: I've lost my wallet = I don't have my wallet; it's still lost.

- If someone says, "I've lost my wallet," you might offer, "Can I help you find it?"

Past simple: I lost my wallet and then I found it under my car seat.

- Both events happened in the past and are finished.

Common mistake: using present perfect with a specific past time

Do not use present perfect when mentioning a past time in proximity.

1. I ~~have seen~~ the movie last week.

Because a specific past time is given, you can't use present perfect. Use past simple:

2. I **saw** the movie last week.

3.4 Present Perfect Continuous

Present perfect continuous is used when the action started in the past and is still ongoing. The starting point in time is typically given. You'll often see for + time or since + time.

Active voice:

1. I **have been living** in Toronto for a year.
2. I'**ve been having** these migraines for two months.
3. I'**ve been having** them since June.
4. I **have been having** them on-and-off for months since the accident.

Passive voice: There is NO PASSIVE VOICE for any perfect continuous.

Present Perfect vs. Present Perfect Continuous

Compare the sentence pairs below. The first example in each pair is in present perfect and deals with distinct experiences; the second is in present perfect continuous and deals with an action that started in the past and is still ongoing.

Present perfect	Present perfect continuous
Have you ever **lived** in Toronto? Yes, I **have lived** in Toronto. Experience Unknown whether the person lives in Toronto	I **have been living** in Toronto for a year. Action that started in the past and is still ongoing
Over the last few weeks, ever since I had that inspiring dream, I'**ve thought of** several solutions to this problem.	Over the last few weeks, ever since we got that lousy new manager, I'**ve been thinking of** quitting my job.
Since the earthquake, we'**ve had** several power outages.	Since the earthquake, we'**ve been having** frequent power outages.

Past Verbs

3.5 Past Simple

Past simple is mainly used for things that happened in the past, that are finished, that are no longer true.

	Passive Voice	**Active Voice**
1st person singular	I **was given** an award for my speech.	The school **gave** me an award for my speech.
2nd person singular or plural	You **were sent** to the office again for bad behaviour!?	The teacher **sent** you to the office again for bad behaviour!?
3rd person singular	The iPad **was damaged** when it **was knocked** off the table.	The kids **damaged** the iPad when they **knocked** it off the table.
1st person plural	We **weren't told** to study this chapter for the test.	The teacher **didn't tell** us to study this chapter for the test.
3rd person plural	They **were kicked out** of the mall for rowdiness.	Mall security **kicked** them **out** of the mall for rowdiness.

Important pronunciation note for *-ed* endings:

In general, the *e* in *ed* is silent unless the word ends in *t* or *d*:

1. Star**ted**
2. En**ded**

With words that end in *t* or *d*, the *e* in *ed* needs to be pronounced in order to clearly enunciate the two consonants at the end. You can't do it without the *e* sound.

3.5A Transform these sentences into their passive forms:

	Passive Voice	**Active Voice**
1st person singular	I ______________________ to the hospital when I broke my leg.	An ambulance **took** me to the hospital when I broke my leg.
2nd person singular or plural	I'm impressed that you ____________________________ an award.	I'm impressed that they **gave** you an award.
3rd person singular	He ____________________________ for bad behaviour.	The teacher **scolded** him for bad behaviour.
1st person plural	We ______________________________ _____ about the changes.	They **didn't tell** us about the changes.
3rd person plural	All the pizza slices ___________________ by the greedy child.	The greedy child **ate** all the pizza slices!

Past Simple vs Present Perfect

Past simple deals with events that are finished. Present perfect deals with experiences. This is important: Don't use present perfect when mentioning a specific past time.

Past simple	**Present perfect**
I **worked** at Omni Mega Group when I was younger. This refers to a **specific past behaviour** that is no longer true.	I**'ve worked** at 3 different companies in this field. This refers to having the **experience** of working at 3 different companies. There is no time information.
I already **dealt** with this last week! Why is it broken again? This refers to a **specific past event**.	I**'ve** never **dealt** with this kind of issue. I'll have to do some research. This refers to lack of **experience**.

3.5B Practice using passive voice. Conjugate these verbs.

Most of these verbs are in past simple, passive voice. One is in present simple, passive voice.

The Mice in Council

The mice **1) (distress)** ______________________ on account of their common enemy the cat, so a council **2) (call)** ______________________ to devise means of ridding themselves of the annoyance.

Many plans **3) (propose)** ______________________ and **4) (reject)** ______________________. At last, **5) (suggest)** ______________________ by a young mouse that a bell be hung round the cat's neck. With advance notice of her coming, they might escape to their holes.

The proposal **6) (hail)** ______________________ with applause and **7) (agree to)** ______________________ unanimously. An old mouse had sat in silence, but just then got up and said, "That is well, but who will bell the cat?" The mice looked at one another, but no one answered.

The old mouse said, "It is easy to advise. What **8) (want)** ______________________ is someone to act."

3.5C Cumulative Review: Passive vs Active: Present Simple, Past Simple, Present Continuous, Present Perfect

This review covers verbs in active and passive voice:

- Present simple
- Past simple
- Present continuous
- Present perfect

Best Study Practices

Research has uncovered several practices that **1) (consistently use)** ______________________ by successful students.

Many students find that having their study sessions in a quiet environment **2) (lead)** ______________________ to better focus and improved retention of information. While studying, **3) (recommend)** ______________________ that students avoid distractions such as social media or television.

In terms of whether it's better to study alone or in a group, a study **4) (conduct)** ______________________ recently which **5) (show)** ______________________ that higher grades **6) (achieve)** ______________________ by those who study in groups at least once a week.

Currently in many schools, innovative learning methods **7) (implement)** ______________________ to enhance student engagement and achievement. For example, flashcards and quizzes **8) (consistently find)** ______________________ to improve learning.

Finally, with regard to physical activity, **9) (find)** ______________________ that many high achievers **10) (balance)** ______________________ study with physical activity. This **11) (prove)** ______________________ that regular exercise breaks during study periods **12) (enhance)** ______________________ productivity and mental alertness.

3.6 Past Continuous

Past continuous is used for interrupted action. The **ongoing action** takes past continuous, and the ***interruption*** takes past simple. You'll often see *while* + past continuous.

I didn't ***pick up*** the phone because I **was eating** dinner.

Active voice	Passive voice
The shippers ***damaged*** the product while they **were unloading** it.	The product ***was damaged*** while it **was being unloaded**.

Important pronunciation note about *being* vs *been*

Being (as in "while it was *being* shipped") is pronounced *bee–ing*. This word has a long pronunciation.

Been (as in "the product has *been* shipped") is pronounced *bin*. This word has a short pronunciation.

Don't use past continuous for no reason:

INCORRECT:	What were you doing last weekend?
CORRECT:	What did you do last weekend?
INCORRECT:	Last weekend, I was just watching TV.
CORRECT:	Last weekend, I just watched TV.

3.6A Use past simple and past continuous to conjugate the verbs in these sentences.

The ongoing action takes past continuous, and the interruption takes past simple:

As I **1) (walk)** ______________________ home, it suddenly **2) (begin)** ______________________ to rain heavily.

While they **3) (watch)** ______________________ the movie, the power **4) (go)** ______________________ out.

He **5) (read)** ______________________ a book when his phone **6) (ring)** ______________________.

While we **7) (drive)** ______________________ through the countryside, we **8) (see)** ______________________ a beautiful sunset.

3.6B Transform these sentences into their passive forms:

Active Voice	Passive Voice
1. The workman broke the window while he was cleaning it.	The window __________ while it __________.
2. Thieves stole the sports car while its owner was storing it for the winter.	The sports car __________ while it __________ for the winter.
3. The archive staff misplaced the documents while they were archiving them.	The documents __________ while they __________.
4. The computer corrupted the data while the IT staff were transferring it to the new system.	The data __________ while it __________ to the new system.
5. Protesters vandalized the painting while a gallery was displaying it.	The painting __________ while it __________.

3.7 Past Perfect

When you have two actions in the past and you want to make it clear that they didn't happen at the same time, the **earlier one** takes past perfect and the ***later one*** takes past simple.

Active voice:

- Before I ***moved*** to China to teach English, I **had worked** at several schools in Canada.
- The staff ***kicked*** the customer out of the store because he **had behaved** rudely.

Passive voice:

- He ***was fired*** because he **had been asked** to improve his sales performance and he couldn't.

3.7A Transform these sentences into their passive forms:

Active Voice	Passive Voice
1. The committee **rejected** the project because the team **hadn't completed** it on time.	The project (reject) __________because it (not complete)__________ on time.
2. She **accepted** the proposal because the experts **had** thoroughly **reviewed** it.	The proposal (accept) __________because it (thoroughly review) __________.
3. The organizers **cancelled** the event because they **had not raised** the necessary funds.	The event (cancel) ________ because the necessary funds (not raise) ________.
4. Although the mechanic **repaired** the machine, the storm **had** severely **damaged** it.	Although the machine (repair) __________, it (severely damage) __________ during the storm.
5. They finally **found** the solution after they **had** unsuccessfully **tried** many alternatives.	The solution (finally find) __________ after many alternatives (unsuccessfully try) __________.
6. They **gave** the award to Dr. Mars because his lab **had made** groundbreaking discoveries.	The award (give) __________ to Dr. Mars because groundbreaking discoveries (make) __________ in his lab.

Active Voice	Passive Voice
7. They **made** the decision hastily after they **had** only **discussed** the problem for a few minutes.	The decision (hastily make) __________ after the problem (only discuss) __________ for a few minutes.
8. They **terminated** the contract because both parties **had not met** the terms.	The contract (terminate) __________ because the terms (not meet) __________ by both parties.

3.8 Past Perfect Continuous vs Past Perfect

Past perfect continuous describes an ongoing action that ended when another action started in the past. In contrast, past perfect deals with an experience that occurred before a more recent experience.

Past Perfect Continuous:	Past Perfect:
Before I ***moved*** to China to teach English, I **had been working** at three schools in Toronto. • ***Past simple*** • **Past perfect continuous** I had three part-time teaching jobs at the same time before I moved to China. This is about an ongoing action that ended when another action started in the past: these three jobs ended and I flew away.	Before I ***moved*** to China to teach English, I **had worked** at several schools in Toronto. • ***Past simple*** • **Past perfect** This is about the experience of being at these schools before moving to China.

Past Perfect Continuous:	Past Perfect:
Q. Before you ***moved*** to Canada, where **had** you **been living**? A. Before I ***moved*** to Canada, I **had been living** in England. • This is about what I'd been doing right before I moved to Canada.	Q. Before you ***moved*** to Canada, where **had** you **lived**? A. Before I ***moved*** to Canada, I **had lived** in Poland and England. • This is about the experience of living in two countries before moving to Canada. I haven't given any information about when I lived in those countries or in which order.

Note: There is NO PASSIVE VOICE for any perfect continuous.

3.8A Past Perfect vs Past Perfect Continuous

1. Match the sentence to its meaning:

a) I had marked the papers when you called.		1) You interrupted my work.
b) I was marking papers when you called.		2) I had finished marking papers for the day.
c) I had been marking papers before you called.		3) I had completed marking the papers.

Conjugate the verbs:

2. Yesterday when I (meet) _______________ Ali, I was so tired because I (cook) _______________ all day.

3. When they finally (arrive) _______________ at the hotel, they looked exhausted as they (drive) _______________ for over ten hours.

4. I wish I (spend) _______________ more time studying before I (write) _______________ that test. I'm very unhappy with my mark.

5. The garden (look) _______________ beautiful because she (take care) _______________ of it all summer.

6. He (realize) _______________ he (lose) _______________ his phone only after he got home

7. When the guests (arrive) _______________ , the house smelled amazing because I _______________ (bake) all afternoon.

8. The climbers were exhausted by the time they (reach) _______________ the summit because they (climb) _______________ since dawn.

9. The streets were wet when we (wake up) _______________ because it (rain) _______________ all night.

10. She (feel) _______________ confident during the interview because she (prepare) _______________ for weeks.

Future Verbs

While there are four future tenses, one of the most commonly used verb tenses for future events is **present continuous**:

- What **are** you **doing** tonight? We**'re playing** basketball.
- What **are** you **doing** next year? I**'m going** to college next year.
- What **are** you **doing** this weekend? We**'re** probably **going** to the zoo.
- Where **are** you **planning** on going to school? I**'m planning** on going to the University of Toronto.

3.9 Future Simple

Purpose	Active voice	Passive voice
Resolving	I **WILL do** it this time!	It **WILL be done** this time!
Promising	I **will do** it tomorrow. I**'ll do** it tomorrow.	It **will be done** tomorrow. It**'ll be done** tomorrow.
Emphasis	I **will clean** it. I**'ll clean** it!	It **will be cleaned**. It**'ll be cleaned**!

3.9A Transform these sentences into their passive forms:

Notice that many of the subjects are too obvious. In these cases, passive voice is an improvement.

	Active Voice	Passive Voice
1.	I **will write** the report by Monday.	The report __________________ by Monday.
2.	They **will announce** the winners next week.	The winners __________________ next week.
3.	We **will plant** new trees in the garden.	New trees __________________ in the garden.
4.	The company **will launch** the new product in June.	The new product __________________ in June.
5.	The chef **will prepare** the meal before the guests arrive.	The meal __________________ before the guests arrive.

	Active Voice	Passive Voice
6.	The students **will clean** the classroom after the session.	The classroom ________________ after the session.
7.	The gardener **will water** the plants every morning.	The plants ________________ every morning.
8.	The teacher **will check** the homework tomorrow.	The homework ________________ tomorrow.
9.	The council **will build** a new playground in the park.	A new playground ________________ in the park.
10.	The scientists **will conduc**t an experiment next week.	An experiment ________________ next week.
11.	The company **will hire** new employees next month.	New employees ________________ next month.
12.	The team **will solve** the problem by the end of the day.	The problem ________________ by the end of the day.

What's the difference between *"going to"* and *"will"*?

Q. What are you going to do?

- This is the most common way of asking.

Q. What will you do?

- This is more formal.
- This is often used in situations where someone has received bad news or is being compelled to do something (by circumstance or a foe).

3.10 Future Continuous

Future continuous is generally used to make a prediction about the future.

Active voice: By this time next year, I**'ll be working** somewhere else.

Passive voice:There is NO PASSIVE VOICE for future continuous.

3.11 Future Perfect

*High up in the north in the land called Svithjod, there stands a rock. It is 100 miles high and 100 miles wide. Once every thousand years, a little bird comes to this rock to sharpen its beak. When the rock has thus been worn away, then a single day of eternity **will have gone by**.*

Henrick van Loon

Future perfect is used to indicate that an action/experience will be finished/ accomplished BY/UP TO/BEFORE some future time. It can be thought of as present perfect from a future perspective.

Present perfect: I'**ve read** almost every Harry Potter book.

Future perfect: If I get that new Harry Potter book, I **will have read** everything by JK Rowling.

By is a big clue that you need to use future perfect:

I hope that **by** next spring, I **will have passed** IELTS.

I have travelled to China, the US, and France. Next year, when I go to England, I **will have visited** four countries.

- I am referring to the experience of visiting these countries.

Active voice	Passive voice:
By this time next year, we'**ll have destroyed** our rivals. This is a prediction that by this time next year AT THE LATEST, our rivals will lose. • We are working on a lot of problems right now, but I think **by** next week, we **will have resolved** most of them.	**By** this time next year, our rivals **will have been destroyed**. Pronunciation: will have been destroyed = *will'uv bin* destroyed • We are working on a lot of problems right now, but I think **by** next week, most of them **will have been resolved**.

3.11A Transform these sentences into their passive forms

Notice that many of the subjects are too obvious. In these cases, passive voice is an improvement.

	Active Voice	Passive Voice
1.	I **will have finished** the assignment by tomorrow.	The assignment ________________ by tomorrow.
2.	The scientists **will have synthesized** a new compound by the end of this month.	A new compound ________________ by the end of this month.
3.	The team **will have completed** the project before the deadline.	The project ________________ before the deadline.
4.	The workers **will have repaired** the road by next week.	The road ________________ by next week.
5.	The chef **will have cooked** the entire meal by 7 PM.	The entire meal ________________ by 7 PM.
6.	We **will have painted** the house by the end of the month.	The house ________________ by the end of the month.
7.	The students **will have submitted** their essays by Friday.	The essays ________________ by Friday.
8.	The scientists **will have analyzed** all the data by next Tuesday.	All the data ________________ by next Tuesday.
9.	The teacher **will have graded** all the exams by tomorrow afternoon.	All the exams ________________ by the teacher by tomorrow afternoon.
10.	I **will have organized** the entire event by next Saturday.	The entire event ________________ by next Saturday.

3.12 Future Perfect Continuous

Purpose: Describing something that starts BEFORE a future point in time AND will also be ongoing at that future point in time

Active voice: I've been here for nine years. By this time next year, I **will have been working** here for 10 years.

Pronunciation: will have been working = *will'uv bin* working

Passive voice: There is NO PASSIVE VOICE for any perfect continuous.

Future Perfect vs Future Perfect Continuous

Experience vs Time

I **have worked** at three different companies in this industry. If I get this new job, I **will have worked** for four different companies in this industry.

- Present perfect (have worked) and future perfect (will have worked) deal with experience.

I **have been working** at Company X for three years. If I stay here for one more year, I **will have been working** here for four years.

- Present perfect continuous (have been working) and future perfect continuous (will have been working) deal with time.

3.12A Use either future perfect or future perfect continuous in these sentences.

1. Assuming I don't get fired, by next month, I (work) ________________ at this company for five years.
2. By 2030 at the latest, humanity (establish) ________________ a permanent base on the moon.
3. By the time he retires, he (teach) ________________ for over 40 years.
4. By tomorrow morning, I (drive) ________________ for ten hours straight.
5. I can't believe this crowd! By the time the movie starts, we (wait) ________________ in line for three hours.
6. I hope that by the end of this year, I (complete) ________________ my degree.
7. If everything goes according to plan, she (finish) ________________ writing her novel by the time her vacation starts.
8. She's committed to getting into this program. By the time she writes her exams next month, she (study) ________________ for six months straight.
9. They (build) ________________ the new bridge by this time next year.
10. They (reach) ________________ their destination by sunset.
11. We (plant) ________________ 100 trees by the end of this week.

4. Complex Sentence Essentials: Subordinate Clauses & Relative Clauses

4.1 Sentence Structure Essentials Review

Let's quickly review the essential components of any sentence.

The basic unit of meaning is a clause. A clause consists of a subject and predicate, and a sentence is composed of one or more clauses.

1. A simple sentence has one independent clause, which just means a clause that makes sense by itself.

The cat caught a mouse.

- Subject = The cat
- Predicate = caught a mouse
  - » The predicate is the verb (caught) + what that verb controls (a mouse).
- This sentence has one independent clause.

2. A compound sentence has two (or more) independent clauses joined together by a coordinating conjunction.

The cat caught a mouse, but it didn't eat it.

- Independent clause #1 = The cat caught a mouse.
- Independent clause #2 = It didn't eat it.
- Coordinating conjunction = but
- This sentence has two independent clauses. We call this a compound sentence.

3. A complex sentence is composed of at least one independent and one dependent clause.

The cat caught a mouse because it likes to hunt.

- Independent clause = The cat caught a mouse.
- Dependent clause = because it likes to hunt
- Subordinating conjunction = because
- This sentence has one independent clause and one dependent clause. We call this a complex sentence.

1. Simple sentence = Independent clause

The technical term for a simple sentence is an *independent clause. Independent* means that it can stand by itself as a sentence – it makes sense on its own.

A clause is a subject and predicate combo:

- A subject is a noun. It's who or what the sentence is about.
- The predicate is the verb + what the verb controls. It's what happens to the subject.

These are the most common structures for independent clauses (i.e., simple sentences):

SUBJECT	**PREDICATE**				
Noun	**Verb**	**Object**	**Complement**	**Adverb**	**Preposition phrase**
Richard	runs.				
Lenny	loves	lasagna.			
Carol	is		crazy.		
Quantum	types			quickly.	
Terry	travels				by train.

2. Compound sentence = Independent clause + independent clause

When we join two or more independent clauses together with a coordinating conjunction, we call it a compound sentence. Conjunctions are joining words.

There are six coordinating conjunctions that we use today*, all of them two and three letter words: but, and, nor, so, or, yet (BAN SOY).

Let's turn our simple sentences into compound sentences:

- Lenny loves lasagna, but he loathes linguine.
- Carol is crazy, and she complains constantly.

**for* is also a coordinating conjunction, but is rarely used as a conjunction today

3. Complex sentence = Independent clause + dependent clause

In both simple sentences and compound sentences, we've been dealing with one or more independent clauses. A simple sentence is a single independent clause. A compound sentence is two or more independent clauses joined together using a coordinating conjunction (BAN SOY: but, and, nor, so, or, yet).

Now let's get to dependent clauses.

Just like an independent clause, a dependent clause also has a subject and a predicate, but it doesn't make sense on its own. That's why it's called a *dependent* clause - it depends on an independent clause for its meaning. The most common type of dependent clause is a subordinate clause. A subordinate clause looks like an independent clause, but it begins with a subordinating conjunction. The most common ones can be remembered by the acronym **SWWAABB**: **s**ince, **w**hen, **w**hile, **a**lthough, **a**fter, **b**efore, **b**ecause.

Independent clause: She runs every day.

- This makes sense on its own.

Dependent clause: *because* she runs every day

- This doesn't make sense on its own.

A dependent clause needs an **independent clause** to make sense:

- **She feels good** because she runs every day.

You can flip the order of the clauses.

- Because she runs every day, **she feels good.**

In this section, we'll look at the two most common kinds of dependent clauses: subordinate clauses and relative clauses. Chapter 7 covers relative clauses in depth.

Note: Both subordinate and relative clauses are **modifiers**. A modifier is a general term for any word, phrase, or clause that doesn't make sense on its own, but which modifies something else. Many of the grammar structures we have looked at so far are modifiers: adjectives, adverbs, preposition phrases, subordinate clauses, and relative clauses.

4.2 Subordinate Clauses

Subordinate clauses are the easiest way to improve your writing. They allow you to add details to almost any part of the sentence.

Subordinate clauses begin with **subordinating conjunctions**. The most commonly used subordinating conjunctions can be remembered by the acronym **SWWAABB:** since, when, while, although, after, before, because.

Subordinate clause | *Subordinating conjunction* / **Independent clause**

- *Since* it might rain, **I brought an umbrella**.
- *Whenever* it rains, **I like to make hot chocolate**.
- **I don't answer the phone** *while* I'm eating dinner.
- *Although* it's raining, **I still want to go out**.
- *Even though* he's really sick, **he still went to work** *because* he's scared of getting fired.

Can You Start a Sentence with *Because*?

The subordinate clause can go before or after the independent clause. If the subordinate clause comes first, place a comma after it. If the subordinate clause comes second, it generally does not need a comma.

- **Because she runs every day,** she feels good.
- She feels good **because she runs every day**.

Subordinating Conjunctions

Subordinate clauses begin with subordinating conjunctions. The most frequently used subordinating conjunctions can be remembered by the acronym **SWWAABB:** since, when, while, although, after, before, because. Here are some others:

- as, as if, as soon as, as though
- at the same time as
- even as, even if
- even though, though
- wherever
- whereas
- whether
- if
- in case
- no matter what
- once
- rather than
- regardless of what
- so that
- unless
- until
- whatever
- whatsoever
- whenever

Subordinate Clause Placement & Punctuation

Subordinate clauses are generally added to the beginning or end of a sentence, but you can also add them in the middle of a sentence. Because it's less common, using them in the middle of a sentence is considered higher level writing. It's cognitively more complicated to understand a sentence when you split the subject and predicate with a long modifier.

If the subordinate clause starts the sentence, put a comma after it. If the subordinate clause follows a short independent clause, you don't need a comma. With a longer independent clause followed by a subordinate clause, it's up to you whether to use a comma after the independent clause. You have to trust your ears: will a comma help the reader understand what's going on?

This is a consistent grammar rule. If you place any modifier before the independent clause, use a comma after it (like in this sentence).

You can HEAR the punctuation. You pause at the comma when reading aloud.

Use your ears:

Adverb	Preposition phrase	Subordinate clause
Yesterday, I went to bed at 11 PM.	**In the final step,** you should write a conclusion.	**Because it's cold,** we're staying in.
I went to bed at 11 PM **yesterday**.	You should write a conclusion **in the final step**.	We're staying in **because it's cold**.

Check out this complex sentence with one **independent clause** and two subordinate clauses. Note how many ways the clauses can be arranged:

1. Because this medicine has toxic side effects, **we don't recommend it** unless the situation is dire.
2. Unless the situation is dire, **we don't recommend this medicine** because it has toxic side effects.
3. Because this medicine has toxic side effects, unless the situation is dire, **we don't recommend it**.
4. Unless the situation is dire, because this medicine has toxic side effects, **we don't recommend it**.
5. **We don't recommend this medicine** because it has toxic side effects, unless the situation is dire.
6. **We don't recommend this medicine** unless the situation is dire because it has toxic side effects.

4.2A Use an appropriate subordinating conjunction in each spot.

You can use each of the common subordinating conjunctions (SWWAABB) once.

- since
- when
- while
- although
- after
- before
- because

The Wolf and the Cat

A wolf ran out of the forest into a village 1) _______________ a huntsman and a pack of hounds were after it.

The wolf saw a cat on a fence and pleaded, "My friend, which of the farmers here is the kindest? I need to hide 2) _______________ my enemies are chasing me."

"Go quickly and ask Stefan," said the cat. "He is a very kind man."

"That's true, 3) _______________ I tore the skin off one of his sheep."

"Well, then, try Demian."

"I'm afraid he's been angry with me, too, 4) _______________ I carried off one of his kids."

"Run over there, then. Trofim lives there."

"Trofim! I'm afraid of even meeting him. He's been threatening to shoot me since the spring 5) _______________ I killed one of his lambs."

"Dear me, that's bad! But perhaps Klim will protect you."

"I doubt he'll protect me 6) _______________ I killed one of his calves earlier this year!"

"You've quarreled with the entire village," said the cat. "What sort of protection can you hope for here? These peasants would have been willing to help you 7) _______________ you attacked their animals, but they are not so devoid of sense as to be willing to save you now. Really, you have only yourself to blame. You're going to reap what you've sown."

4.3 Relative Clauses = Adjective Clauses

The second most common type of independent clause is a relative clause. It's called a relative clause because it's related to the thing right before it. In many grammar textbooks, it's referred to as an adjective clause. Here's the difference:

- Adjectives come right BEFORE the noun they describe.
- Relative clauses come right AFTER the noun or idea they describe.

Adjective	I have a **big** dog.
Relative clause	I have a dog **that is big**.

Relative Pronouns

Most relative clauses begin with these relative pronouns: who, that, which, where.

Use WHO for specific people:

- Jessie, who lives next door, is coming over on the weekend.

Use THAT/WHO for general people:

- My friend that/who lives next door is coming over on the weekend.

Use THAT/WHICH for general things:

- The part that/which I ordered last month has finally arrived.

Use WHERE for places:

- That's the town where I grew up.

Punctuation in Relative Clauses

If the information in the relative clause is needed to understand who/what the preceding noun is about, don't use commas. If the information in the relative clause is not needed to understand who/what the preceding noun is about but is an extra detail, use commas.

In these examples, the information in the <u>relative clause</u> IS needed to understand who/what the **preceding noun** is about.

- **My friend** <u>that/who lives next door</u> is coming over on the weekend.
  - » Without the information in the relative clause, the reader doesn't know which friend you're talking about.
- **The part** <u>that/which I ordered last month</u> has finally arrived.
  - » Without the information in the relative clause, the reader doesn't know which part you're talking about.
- That's the **town** <u>where I grew up</u>.
  - » "Where I grew up" tells the reader why you are referring to this town.

Sometimes relative clauses are inside commas, and sometimes they're not:

In these examples, the information in the <u>relative clause</u> is NOT needed to understand who/what the **preceding noun** is about.

- **Jessie**, who lives next door, is coming over on the weekend.
  - » The reader knows Jessie is coming over. The fact that Jessie lives next door is an extra detail.
- **The X501**, which I ordered last month, has finally arrived.
  - » The reader knows which specific part you ordered. The fact that it was ordered last month is an extra detail.
- That's **Toronto**, <u>where I grew up</u>.
  - » "Toronto" is specific. "Where I grew up" is an extra detail.

4.3A Use a relative pronoun in each spot.

Use these relative pronouns:

- who
- that
- which

The Goose with the Golden Eggs

A villager had the good fortune to possess a goose **1)** ________________ laid her a golden egg each day of the year.

After a while, the woman, **2)** _______________ had become impatient with so slow an income, killed the goose to get all at once the gold **3)** _______________ she thought was inside.

When she cut her open, she was disappointed to find nothing special inside the body of the goose, **4)** _______________ looked exactly like the body of any other goose.

Those **5)** _______________ try to get too much can lose it all.

4.3B Use relative clauses to combine the simple sentences in this fable into complex sentences.

The Miser

1. A miser sold all that he had and bought a lump of gold. He buried the gold in a hole in the ground and went to look at it daily.

- Transform the second sentence into a relative clause.

____

____

____

____

2. One of his workmen observed his frequent visits to the spot. The workman decided to watch his movements.

- Transform the second sentence into a relative clause. Place this relative clause inside the first sentence after “workmen” because a relative clause needs to go directly after the idea it’s related to.

____

____

____

____

3. He soon discovered the secret of the hidden treasure, dug down, and found the lump of gold. He stole the lump of gold.

- Transform the second sentence into a relative clause.

4. The miser found the hole empty on his next visit. He began to tear his hair and wail.

- Transform the first sentence into a relative clause. Keep "The miser" at the beginning.

5. A neighbor asked him why he was so upset. The neighbour saw him overcome with grief,

- Transform the second sentence into a relative clause. Place this relative clause inside the first sentence after "neighbour" because a relative clause needs to go directly after the idea it's related to.

6. After he learned what had happened, the neighbour said, "Don't be sad. Put a stone in the hole and pretend that the gold is still lying there. It will do you the same amount of good, because when the gold was there, you didn't make the slightest use of it."

- Transform the third sentence into a relative clause.

____

____

____

____

4.4 The Most Powerful Sentence Structure

This is the hardest-working complex sentence template because it allows you to include cause, effect, and significance in one sentence. It's composed of an **independent clause**, <u>subordinate clause</u>, and *relative clause*.

- <u>Because this barbeque folds up into a small case</u>, **you can bring it with you anywhere**, *which means you can turn any trip to the park into an amazing picnic.*
  - <u>Cause</u> + **effect** + *benefit/significance.*

You can put a lot of information into one sentence. Here's another example:

- <u>Because it's raining</u>, **we'll stay indoors today**, *which means we can watch a movie.*
  - <u>The subordinate clause is the cause</u>.
  - **The independent clause is the effect.**
  - *The relative clause explains the significance.*

In this single sentence structure, you've got cause-effect-consequence:

- <u>Because the weather is fantastic</u>, **we'll spend time in the garden**, *which means we can plant our herbs.*
  - <u>Subordinate clause</u> + **independent clause** + *relative clause.*
  - <u>Cause</u> + **effect** + *significance.*

4.4A Use subordinate and relative clauses to combine the simple sentences in this fable into complex sentences.

The Piglet, the Sheep, and the Goat

1. A young pig was shut up in a farmyard with a goat and a sheep. He grunted and squeaked and resisted violently. The shepherd tried to lay hold of him.

- Transform the first sentence into a relative clause. Keep "A young pig" at the beginning.
- Transform the third sentence into a subordinate clause.

2. The sheep and the goat complained of his cries. The sheep and the goat are often handled by the farmer and do not protest. They found his cries distressing.

- Transform the second sentence into a relative clause. Place it inside the first sentence after "The sheep and the goat."
- Transform the third sentence into a relative clause.

3. To this the pig replied, "Our situations are very different. He catches you only for your wool or your milk. However, he lays hold of me for my very life."

- Transform the second and third sentences into subordinate clauses.

4.5 Common Sentence Structure Problems

4.5.1 Sentence Fragment (SF)

Fragment = a (small) piece of a whole

A sentence fragment (SF) is part of a sentence – it's not a complete sentence. These are fragments:

- SF Because it was cold.
- SF In the morning.

Neither of these makes sense on its own:

- "Because it was cold" is a dependent clause.
- "In the morning" is a preposition phrase.

They need an **independent clause** to make sense:

- Because it was cold, **I wore a sweater.**
- In the morning, **I eat breakfast.**

4.5.2 Run-on Sentence (ROS)

A run-on sentence (ROS) breaks the rules of how we can put clauses together: you can't join two independent clauses together using a comma (or nothing at all). The table below shows four solutions to a run-on sentence. The 4th solution is covered in Unit 6: Semicolons and Conjunctive Adverbs.

I ordered jewelry, ROS it turned out to be fake.

Solution 1: Use a period.	I ordered jewelry**.** It turned out to be fake.
Solution 2: Use a **coordinating conjunction**.	I ordered jewelry, **but** it turned out to be fake.
Solution 3: Transform one of the independent clauses into a **dependent clause** (subordinate or relative clause), which gives you a complex sentence.	I ordered jewelry **although it turned out to be fake**. I ordered jewelry **that/which** ~~it~~ **turned out to be fake**.
Solution 4: Use a semi-colon + conjunctive adverb + comma combo.	I ordered jewelry**; however,** it turned out to be fake.

4.5.3 Parallelism in Comparisons

When making a comparison, both items in the comparison need to have the same grammatical form to maintain parallelism. If the items are not grammatically parallel, the result is a syntax error, an apples-and-oranges comparison.

4.5.3A Parallel Structure in Comparisons - Fix the Errors (Level 2)

1. Mia's slice of cake is large while Jenny is small.
2. In many rich countries, the food quality is worse than poor countries.
3. I believe work experience is equal to or sometimes more valuable than educated people.
4. Italy's land area is about 294,000 square kilometers while Spain is about 499,000 square kilometers.

4.5.3B Parallel Structure in Comparisons - Fix the Errors (Level 3)

1. When you get older, you will need to face more challenging work than your previous school years.
2. High schools in China apply class rankings to compare students' grades with their classmates.
3. According to research by universities, cheating incidents in 2019 were 50% more common than the year before.
4. Many social media users only post the best parts of their life, which may make children think that their lives are not as good as others.
5. The only problem with my new place is that the kitchen is smaller than my previous place.
6. People in big cities have more flexibility in their careers compared to small cities.
7. People with good communication skills are 70% more likely to get promoted than those who do not.

5. Conditional Subordinate Clauses

Conditional subordinate clauses start with *if*.

Real conditional describes real possibilities, but unreal conditional is often used for hopes, warnings, and regrets.

5.1 Real Conditional

Real conditional is most commonly used to describe causes and effects. It describes a situation that can happen if another situation happens first. Most computer coding is an example of real conditional:

- If A does Y, then B does Z.

The **verb** in the *if* clause is in present simple.	The **verb** in the *then* clause is in...	
If you **overcook** vegetables,	they **lose** their flavour.	1) **present simple** for facts or cause-effect relationships
If you **finish** your homework,	you **can play** video games.	2) **modal present** (can be, should/ must be + passive) for permission or possibility
If this interview **goes** well, If you **overcook** these vegetables,	I'**ll get** the job. they **will lose** their flavour.	3) **future simple** for predictions or outcomes

5.2 Unreal Conditional – Present

Unreal conditional sounds like the opposite of what it means. It's an alternative way to express complaints, regret, guilt, hope, wishes, warnings, or advice:

Complaints

1. If he practiced more, he would get better results.

- If he practised more = he doesn't practice enough
- he would get better results = he isn't getting satisfactory results

2. If she behaved, she wouldn't be in the principal's office all the time.

- If she behaved = she doesn't behave
- she wouldn't be in the principal's office all the time = she is in the principal's office all the time

3. If we weren't stuck in this awful traffic jam, we could make it to the meeting on time.

- If we weren't stuck in this traffic jam = we are stuck in this traffic jam
- we could make it to the meeting on time = we can't make it to the meeting on time

4. If the quality were better, I would buy it.

- If the quality were better = the quality isn't good enough
- I would buy it = I'm not going to buy it

Wishes

5. If my supervisor were here, he would know what to do.

- If my supervisor were here = my supervisor is not here
- he would know what to do = no one here knows what to do

6. If I had a billion dollars, I would buy an island.

- If I had $1 billion = I don't have $1 billion
- I would buy = I'm not buying an island because the other half of this statement (If I had $1 billion) isn't true.
- In this case, HAD is NOT past tense. IF + HAD = PRESENT UNREAL

We often say:

- If I were the president, I would....
- If I won the lottery, I would...

Warnings/advice

7. If I were you, I wouldn't do that!

- If I were you = I'm not you
- I wouldn't do that = don't do that

8. If I were you, I wouldn't say that to the boss.
    - If I were you = I'm not you
    - I wouldn't say that to the boss = don't say that to the boss
9. If I were you, I wouldn't wear that to the meeting.
    - If I were you = I'm not you
    - I wouldn't wear that to the meeting = don't wear that to the meeting
10. If your parents knew what you're doing, they'd be furious!
    - If your parents knew what you're doing = your parents have no idea what you're doing
    - they'd be furious = they're calm right now

5.2A Conjugate these verbs using present unreal conditional.

1. If I (win) ________________ the lottery, I (buy) ________________ a sports car.
2. If I (be) ________________ you, I (not eat) ________________ that stinky shrimp.
3. If it (not be) ________________ so cold, we (can go) ________________ outside.
4. If I (not be) ________________ so tired, I (be) ________________ more productive.
5. I (probably meet) ________________ more people if I (not spend) ________________ all my time playing video games.
6. If the government (introduce) ________________ a tax on all plastic bags in supermarkets, this (start) ________________ to add up and people (notice) it by the time they (get) ________________ to the cash register. Then, people (think) ________________ about the amount of plastic they use when buying food and this (lead) ________________ to less garbage being produced.
7. I (get) ________________ higher marks if I (study) ________________ more.

8. If the weather (be) ______________ nice, we (go) ______________ for a walk.
9. She's not doing too well. If she (have) ______________ proper medical treatment, she (recover) ______________ quickly.
10. If it (be) ______________ summer, we (can spend) ______________ more time outside.
11. I (meet) ______________ more people if I (go out) ______________ instead of spending all my time online.

Real vs Unreal Conditional: Compare These Sentence Pairs

Real conditional	Unreal conditional
If I'm promoted, I will make many changes in company policy. • Meaning: I have applied and might be promoted.	If I were promoted, I would make many changes in company policy. • Meaning: I have not applied, and my statement represents advice/wishful thinking.
If you show up to class more often, you will get better marks. • Meaning: a warning and an opportunity to improve	If you showed up to class more often, you would get better marks. • Meaning: You don't show up to class often enough. As a result, you get poor marks.

Don't Confuse Past Tense & Unreal Conditional

The construction of present unreal conditional looks like past tense, but it's not. Putting *if* at the beginning changes things to unreal conditional.

Neutral statement	Unreal conditional - wish/complaint
The weather is not nice, so we won't go for a walk.	If the weather were nice, we would go for a walk. If the weather were nice = the weather is not nice we would go for a walk = we won't go for a walk

Note: BOTH statements provide the exact same information.

5.3 Unreal Conditional – Past

Past unreal conditional describes imaginary situations in the past. This is often the language of regret:

1. If I **had been** there at the meeting, I **could have** properly **explained** how to fix the problem.

- Meaning: I wasn't there. How to fix the problem was not properly explained.

2. He **would not have quit** his job if **he'd thought** there was any chance of smoothing things over with his boss.

- Meaning: He did quit his job. He didn't think there was any chance of smoothing things over.

3. She **would never have hit** the bully if she**'d believed** the school would protect her.

- Meaning: She did hit the bully. She did not believe the school would protect her.

Formula

Note: Either half can go first.

1st **half:** Past unreal conditional looks like past perfect. It uses the same form of the verb and the same helper verb (had) for all subjects:	2nd **half:** Could/would + have + 3rd form of verb (again, there is only one form of the verb for all subjects)
If I **had been** there,	I **could have helped** them.
If you **had worn** warmer clothes,	you **would**n't **have gotten** frost bite.
If they **had**n't **eaten** that old sushi,	they **would**n't **have gotten** food poisoning.

Pronunciation

- If they'd only listened to me, I **could have** helped them. = I **could'uv** helped them
- If you'd worn gloves, you **wouldn't have** gotten frost bite. = you **wood'en'uv** gotten frost bite

5.3A Conjugate these verbs using past unreal conditional.

1. If you (show up) ________________ on time, we (not be) ________________ late.
2. The meeting was cancelled. If I (know) ________________ earlier, I (sleep in) ________________ .
3. No, I didn't end up buying a real Burberry. If it (be) ________________ cheaper, I (get) ________________ it. I ended up getting a knockoff instead for a fraction of the price.

   That's a really nice one! If you (not tell) ________________ me it's a fake, I (never guess) ________________.
4. My project partners were so lazy. I (be) ________________ better off doing the project alone.
5. The hack (not happen) ________________ if he (have) ________________ a stronger password than "ABC123."
6. She is now a successful art teacher and she (might not develop) ________________ this skill if she (not have) ________________ such great teachers.
7. If my father (not push) ________________ me to get a job, I (might not learn) ________________ the value of hard work at such a young age.
8. If he (never change) ________________ his career, his business (stop be successful) ________________ successful and he (not discover) ________________ a passion for what he's doing now.
9. If I (not oversleep) ________________ this morning, I (not miss) ________________ my bus.

5.4 Unreal Conditional – Past & Present

Unreal conditional blends (past and present) describe the present consequences of past mistakes:

If I **had been** there at the meeting, we **wouldn't have** this problem now.

- Past unreal + present unreal
- Meaning: I wasn't at the meeting (past). As a result, we now have a problem (present).

Compare these sentence pairs

Whether to use unreal present or unreal past depends on your meaning:

Past + Present Unreal	Past + Past Unreal
If I had been there, we wouldn't have this problem **now**.	If I had been there, we wouldn't have had this problem **last week**.

Note: For the past, it doesn't make sense to say, "if I had been you." We still use the present form "if I were you." Alternatively, you can say "if I had been in your shoes" (past unreal) or "if it had been me" (past unreal).

1. I can't believe you said that at the meeting yesterday! If I **were** you, I **wouldn't have said** that.

- Present unreal, past unreal

2. I can't believe you said that at the meeting yesterday! If I **had been** in your shoes, I **wouldn't have said** that.

- Past unreal, past unreal

5.4A Conjugate these verbs using past and present unreal conditional.

Use both past and present unreal conditional in each sentence.

1. If I (know) _______________ what I know now, I (not be) _______________ in this mess.

2. If it (not be) _______________ for this traffic jam, we (arrive) _______________ at the conference an hour ago.
3. If I (buy) _______________ those Google shares when Google was brand new, I definitely (not work) _______________ at this crappy job.
4. If I (not eat) _______________ that stinky shrimp for lunch earlier today, I (not have) _______________ a horrible stomachache right now.
5. If I (not quit) _______________ my job, I (not have) _______________ my own business now.
6. I (be) _______________ better prepared for this test tomorrow if I (study) _______________ more over the past few weeks.
7. If I (not party) _______________ in Las Vegas last weekend, I (not be) _______________ broke now.

6. Semicolon + Conjunctive Adverb Sentences

"We cannot control all that happens to us; ***however,*** *we can choose to be in control of our responses."*

- Lionel Kendrick, Mormon leader

"The art of healing comes from nature, not from the physician; ***therefore,*** *the physician must start from nature, with an open mind."*

- Paracelsus

In this complex sentence pattern, the semicolon functions like a period. Wherever you see a semicolon in these examples, you can use a period instead.

The semi-colon signals a more complicated relationship between independent clauses than that signaled by coordinating conjunctions (BAN SOY: but, and, nor, so, or, yet). Typically, the second clause expands on the first clause or provides clarifying details, contrasts with the first clause, or describes a consequence.

- Prof. Davis

Formula

Semi-colon sentences follow this formula:

IC; CA, IC.

Independent clause	semicolon	conjunctive adverb	comma	independent clause	period

> Two important points to remember with semi-colon sentences:

1. BOTH SIDES of the semi-colon MUST BE independent clauses. Each half of the semi-colon sentence must be a sentence on its own.
2. The conjunctive adverb is followed by a comma.

Conjunctive Adverbs and Phrases

Conclusion

- ...; therefore,...
- ...; thus,...

Clarification

- ...; in fact,...
- ...; to clarify, ...
- ...; accordingly, ...

Comparison

- ...; in comparison, ...
- ...; likewise,...
- ...; similarly,...

Contrast

- ...; conversely,...
- ...; however,...
- ...; in contrast, ...
- ...; instead,...
- ...; on the other hand,...
- ...; meanwhile, ...
- ...; otherwise,...

Emphasis

- ...; besides, ...
- ...; notably,...

Regardless

- ...; despite that,...
- ...; in spite of that,...
- ...; nevertheless,...
- ...; nonetheless,...
- ...; regardless,...

Result

- ...; as a result,...
- ...; consequently,...
- ...; thus,...
- ...; therefore,...
- ...; hence,...

Sequence

- ...; additionally, ...
- ...; as well,...
- ...; eventually,...
- ...; finally,...
- ...; furthermore,...
- ...; in addition,...
- ...; meanwhile,...
- ...; moreover,...
- ...; next,...
- ...; subsequently,...

Then is a conjunctive adverb.

One of the most common mistakes involves using *then* like a coordinating conjunction (BANSOY: but, and, nor, so, or, yet):

- We ate dinner, ROS then we had dessert.

This is a run-on sentence (ROS). You can't use *then* to join two independent clauses. To join independent clauses, use *and then* or a semicolon:

- Solution #1: We ate dinner **and then** we had dessert.
- Solution #2: We ate dinner**; then,** we had dessert.

6.1A Use an appropriate conjunctive adverb to complete each sentence.

More than one option is possible for many of these.

1. The hare boasted about his speed; ________________, the tortoise's steady pace won the race in the end.
2. The lion spared the mouse's life; ________________, the mouse later freed the lion from a hunter's net.
3. The ant worked hard all summer storing food; ________________, the grasshopper sang and danced without a care.
4. The fox praised the crow's singing; ________________, when replying, the crow dropped the cheese, and the fox quickly snatched it up.
5. The dog barked at his reflection in the water; ________________, he lost the bone he was carrying in his mouth.
6. The thirsty crow found a pitcher with a little water; ________________, he dropped pebbles into it until the water rose high enough to drink.

7. The peacock flaunted his beautiful feathers; _______________, the crane flew gracefully above, unimpressed by the display.
8. The wolf disguised himself in sheep's clothing to blend in with the flock; _______________, the shepherd discovered the ruse and chased him away.
9. The boy cried "wolf" too many times as a joke; _______________, when a real wolf appeared, no one came to his aid.
10. The farmer discovered that the goose laid golden eggs; _______________, in his greed, he killed the goose, finding no more gold inside.

6.1.3 Run-on Sentences (ROS) and Sentence Fragments (SF) due to Mixing Up Conjunctions

One of the most common reasons for run-on sentences and sentence fragments is mixing up conjunctive adverbs with coordinating or subordinating conjunctions.

Coordinating conjunctions	Subordinating conjunctions	Conjunctive adverbs
Coordinating conjunctions join independent clauses. Coordinating conjunctions are NOT followed by a comma.	Subordinating conjunctions begin subordinate clauses. These are dependent clauses that need an independent clause to make sense. Subordinating conjunctions are NOT followed by a comma.	Conjunctive adverbs begin an independent clause after either a period or semi-colon. In both cases, a comma follows the conjunctive adverb.
I need to go to the mall, **and** I need to get groceries.	**While** I need to go to the mall, I also need to get groceries.	I need to go to the mall; **also,** I need to get groceries.
I've made a lot of progress on the project, **but** it's not done yet.	I've made a lot of progress on the project **although** it's not done yet.	I've made a lot of progress on the project; **however,** it's not done yet.

Conjunction Confusion Consequences

1. If you use a subordinating conjunction instead of a conjunctive adverb, you end up with a sentence fragment:

- SF **Although** it's too big.

Solution:

You either need to add an independent clause or you can replace *Because* with *However,* which is a **conjunctive adverb**:

- **However,** it's too big.

2. If you use a conjunctive adverb instead of a coordinating/subordinating conjunction, you end up with a run-on sentence:

- ROS We went out to a new pizza restaurant the other day, unfortunately it wasn't very good.

Solutions:

1. Use a coordinating conjunction:

- We went out to a new pizza restaurant the other day, **but** it wasn't very good.

2. Use a subordinating conjunction:

- We went out to a new pizza restaurant the other day **although** it wasn't very good.

3. Use a semi-colon + conjunctive adverb pattern:

- We went out to a new pizza restaurant the other day**; unfortunately,** it wasn't very good.

7. Relative Clauses

A relative clause is related to the thing or idea right before it. It's sometimes referred to as an adjective clause. Here's the difference:

- An adjective is placed directly BEFORE the noun it describes.
- A relative clause goes right AFTER the noun or idea it describes.

Adjective	I have a **big** dog.
Relative clause	I have a dog **that is big**.

This chapter will cover five types of relative clauses. Type #1 is, by far, the most common.

7.1 Relative Clause Type #1: Who, That, Which, Where

Type #1 relative clauses most often start with the relative pronouns *who, that, which*, and *where*. These relative clauses are used to give an important detail about the preceding person, place, thing, or idea (i.e. nouns). In general, if you're referring to a person, use *who*. For anything else, you can usually use *which*.

- My friend **who lives in Montreal** is visiting next weekend.
- The memory card**, which I ordered last month,** has finally arrived.

Relative clauses also frequently refer to the entire preceding clause. These often start with *which means* or *which indicates*:

- The patient has a high fever and headache, **which means he might have covid**.
- ..., which might lead to...
- ..., which could result in...

This is the town **where he grew up**.

- **where he grew up** is related to *the town*.
- **where = in which** (we'll see this in 7.3 Type III Relative Clauses)

Who or whom?

Whom or *who*? If in doubt, use *who*. Usage of *whom* is declining and this word will probably become obsolete.

In general, though, if the pronoun/noun you're replacing is a subject noun (i.e. he/she/they), use **who**.

If the pronoun/noun you're replacing is an object noun (i.e. him/her/them), use **whom**.

	Simple sentences	Relative clauses
Who	Jeff will be joining us for lunch. **He** works upstairs.	Jeff, **who** works upstairs, will be joining us for lunch.
Whom	Jeff will be joining us for lunch. **We** met **him** at the party last month.	Jeff, **whom we** met at the party last month, will be joining us for lunch.
Who	Jeff will be joining us for lunch. **He** met **us** at the party last month.	Jeff, **who** met **us** at the party last month, will be joining us for lunch

Punctuation: Defining vs. Non-Defining Relative Clauses

Relative clauses are sometimes surrounded by commas, but often they appear without them. This depends on whether the information in the relative clause is A) needed to understand what the preceding idea is about or B) an extra detail.

A) Defining Relative Clauses for Necessary Information

If the information in the relative clause is crucial for understanding what the preceding idea is about, then DO NOT use commas. These are called ***defining relative clauses***.

- The part **that I ordered last month** has finally arrived.

If you remove "that I ordered last month," the reader doesn't know which part you're talking about:

- The part has finally arrived.

Which part? In this case, it's called a defining relative clause because you need the information in the relative clause to understand what's going on, to "define" *the part*.

With a defining relative clause, you can use *that* or *which*.

- The part **<u>that</u> I ordered last month** has finally arrived.
- The part **<u>which</u> I ordered last month** has finally arrived.

DO NOT PUT COMMAS around a defining relative clause.

B) Non-Defining Relative Clauses for Extra Details

If the information in the relative clause is an extra detail, put the relative clause inside commas. These are called ***non-defining relative clauses***.

In the example below, you can remove the relative clause and the reader will still know what you're talking about.

- Harry Potter 3**, which I ordered last month,** has finally arrived!

Harry Potter 3 is a specific item and "which I ordered last month" is a non-critical detail. In this case, it's a non-defining relative clause.

- Harry Potter 3 has finally arrived!

DO NOT USE THAT with a non-defining relative clause:

Harry Potter 3, ~~that~~ which **I ordered last month,** has finally arrived.

Compare these sentence pairs:

Non-Defining Relative Clause	Defining Relative Clause
Richie**, who sat next to me in grade 9 geography,** became a successful businessman.	The guy **who sat next to me on the plane** is a famous musician.
The X501**, which we bought last month,** has broken down already.	The machine **that/which we bought last month** has broken down already.

Use your ears!

Read your writing aloud as if you were reading a story to children. If you feel the need to pause in order to improve clarity for a listener, you probably need a comma there.

Omitting Relative Pronouns

If you have a defining relative clause with a subject after the relative pronoun, you can omit the relative pronoun. This doesn't work in non-defining relative clauses (the ones that are inside commas).

Example 1:

Simple sentences	You'd lent the file to Larry. The file is on your desk.
Relative clause	The file **<u>that you</u>'d lent to Larry** is on your desk. • ***that*** is the relative pronoun • ***you*** *is the* subject of the verb ('d lent = had lent) in the relative clause • You can omit ***that***. The file **you'd lent to Larry** is on your desk.
Common mistake	The file **that you'd lent** ~~it~~ **to Larry** is on your desk. The file **you'd lent** ~~it~~ **to Larry** is on your desk.

Example 2:

Simple sentences	You got the food from that new place? Was the food any good?
Relative clause	Was the food **that you got from that new place** any good? • ***that*** is the relative pronoun • ***you*** *is the* subject of the verb (got) in the relative clause • You can omit ***that***. Was the food **you got from that new place** any good?
Common mistake	Was the food **that you got** ~~it~~ **from that new place** any good? Was the food **you got** ~~it~~ **from that new place** any good?

Example 3:

Simple sentences	Chen gave me the USB. I can't find it.
Relative clause	I can't find the USB **that Chen gave (to) me**. • ***that*** is the relative pronoun • ***Chen*** *is the* subject of the verb (gave) in the relative clause • You can omit ***that***. I can't find the USB **Chen gave (to) me**.
Common mistake	I can't find the **USB that Chen gave it (to) me.** I can't find the USB **Chen gave it (to) me.**

7.1A Transform these simple sentence pairs into complex sentences using Type I Relative Clauses.

1. The cat is sitting on the windowsill. It is watching the birds outside.

____

____

2. Marisse read a book last night. It was extremely interesting.

____

____

3. My friend moved to New York last year. He is visiting us next weekend.

____

____

4. The old tree has been there for over a hundred years. It's in the middle of the park.

____

____

5. She chose a dress for her performance. It sparkled under the lights.

____

____

6. Gennady teaches mathematics. He is known for his engaging lessons.

____

____

7. This is the restaurant. It received the best reviews in town.

____

____

8. He found a wallet. It belonged to someone in the next building.

____

____

9. We watched a movie last night. It was based on a true story.

10. Dr. Mars won the award. He is known for his groundbreaking research.

7.2 Relative Clause Type #2: Possessive (Whose)

The second type of relative clause begins with the possessive relative pronoun *whose* for both people and things. You use this form in situations where you have a possessive pronoun:

John is upset. + **His** bike was stolen. = John, **whose** bike was stolen, is upset.

possessive pronoun

possessive relative pronoun

1. The company has gone out of business. We bought **their** parts last year.

- The company **whose parts we bought last year** has gone out of business.

2. I'd like to thank John. **His help** was indispensable in getting this project finished on time.

- I'd like to thank John**, whose help** was indispensable in getting this project finished on time.

3. I'd like to thank the members of the public. **Their tips** were crucial in finding the killer.

- I'd like to thank the members of the public**, whose tips** were crucial in finding the killer.

Defining/Non-Defining Relative Clauses

Just like with Type #1 relative clauses, we have defining and non-defining possessive relative clauses. Compare these two sentences:

Defining possessive relative clause	Non-defining possessive relative clause
The customer **whose order we lost** is really mad.	Frank, whose order we lost, is really mad.
Because the subject (the customer) is nonspecific, the information in the relative clause is needed to understand who we are talking about.	Because the subject (Frank) is specific, the relative clause goes between commas. We still know that this is about Frank without the information in the relative clause.
When you read this aloud, there are no pauses.	When you read this aloud, you pause naturally where the commas are.

7.2A Transform these simple sentence pairs into complex sentences using Type II Relative Clauses.

1. The girl is calling for her cat to come down. Her cat climbed the tallest tree in the neighborhood.

____

____

2. I met a museum curator. His passion for ancient history inspired several generations of children.

____

____

3. She borrowed a book from the library. Its pages were almost a hundred years old.

____

____

4. The teacher received an award for excellence in teaching. His lessons are always engaging.

____

____

5. The artist Yasho's work is displayed in the city gallery. He is known for his abstract paintings.

____

____

6. We visited a museum. Its collection of artifacts spans over two thousand years.

____

____

7. She wore a dress. Its fabric shimmered under the ballroom lights.

____

____

8. This bakery attracts customers from all over town. Its bread is known for its authentic French taste.

____

____

7.3 Relative Clause Type #3: Preposition + Whom, Which

In some cases, a relative clause will end in a preposition. You can often move this preposition in front of the relative pronoun to improve clarity.

Prepositions are the small words that come before nouns:

- **under** the table
- **to** Frank
- **after** lunch
- **in, on, over, before, after, through, into**

Simple sentences	That's the table. I left my bag under it.
Complex sentence with *relative clause* ending with a *preposition*	That's the table ***which I left my bag under***.
You can move the *preposition* in front of the *relative pronoun*	That's the table ***under which I left my bag***.

In modern English, you can put the preposition before the relative pronoun or at the end of the relative clause.

Traditionally, the preposition goes before the relative pronoun. A preposition is literally a word that goes before a place:

- *pre* = before
- *position* = place

Simple sentences	Frank is the guy. You should give the file to him.
Complex sentence with *relative clause* ending with a *preposition*	Frank is the guy ***whom you should give the file to***.
You can move the *preposition* in front of the *relative pronoun*	Frank is the guy ***to whom you should give the file***.
Omitting relative pronouns: If you have a defining relative clause (the kind with no commas) with a subject after the ***relative pronoun***, you can omit the relative pronoun.	Frank is the guy ***you should give the file to***. Notice that you can't omit the relative pronoun if you put the preposition ahead of the relative clause: ~~Frank is the guy ***to you*** should give the file.~~

Simple sentences	We have to solve this problem first. After we solve this problem, we can deal with the other issue.
Complex sentence with *relative clause* ending with a *preposition*	In this case, we can't put the preposition at the end of the relative clause.
You can move the *preposition* in front of the *relative pronoun*	We have to solve this problem first, ***after which we can deal with the other issue***.

Simple sentences	That's the lady. You need to send the package to her.
Complex sentence with *relative clause* ending with a *preposition*	That's the lady ***whom you need to send the package to***.

You can move the *preposition* in front of the *relative pronoun*	That's the lady ***to whom* *you need to send the package***.
Omitting relative pronouns: If you have a defining relative clause (the kind with no commas) with a subject after the ***relative pronoun*** (...whom you...), you can omit the relative pronoun.	That's the lady ***you need to send the package to***. Notice that you can't omit the relative pronoun if you put the preposition ahead of the relative clause: ~~That's the lady *to you* need to send the package.~~

Simple sentences	That's the equipment. We need to work with that equipment.
Complex sentence with *relative clause* ending with a *preposition*	That's the equipment ***which* *we need to work with***.
You can move the *preposition* in front of the *relative pronoun*	9. That's the equipment ***with which* *we need to work***.
Omitting relative pronouns: If you have a defining relative clause (the kind with no commas) with a subject after the ***relative pronoun***, you can omit the relative pronoun.	10. That's the equipment ***we need to work with***. Notice that you can't omit the relative pronoun if you put the preposition ahead of the relative clause: 11. ~~That's the equipment with we need to work.~~

7.3A Transform these simple sentence pairs into complex sentences using Type III Relative Clauses.

1. Thank you for your help. Without it, I couldn't have finished this project.

____

____

2. I don't remember the man. I got the message from him.

____

____

3. I can't remember the supplier. We got that part from them last year.

4. That's the village. I grew up in that village.

5. That's the farm. I grew up on that farm.

6. He showed me the powerful computer. He designs his complex architectural models on it.

7. They moved to a new city. They knew very little about it.

8. She passed on the message to her colleague Steve. She collaborates on important projects with him.

9. He found a wallet. There was a rare old coin inside it.

____

____

10. That's the old alleyway. We used to play there as children.

____

____

Expressions: Preposition Phrase + Which/Whom

thanks to which

I'd like to thank our wonderful president for her leadership. **Thanks to her leadership**, we were able to exceed all of our targets.

- I'd like to thank our wonderful president for her leadership, **thanks to which** we were able to exceed all of our targets.

thanks to whom (singular & plural)

I'd like to thank John. T**hanks to him**, we were able to finish this project on time.

- I'd like to thank John, **thanks to whom** we were able to finish this project on time.

I'm grateful for the help provided by everyone in John's department. **Thanks to them,** we were able to locate the records more quickly.

- I'm grateful for the help provided by everyone in John's department**,** **thanks to whom** we were able to locate the records more quickly.

due to which

There's been a big change in the market. **Due to this change,** we can longer do things the same way.

- There's been a big change in the market, **due to which** we can longer do things the same way.

as a result of which

This is the problem. **As a result of this problem,** our project will be delayed.

- This is the problem**, as a result of which** our project will be delayed.

according to whom

The police spoke with the witness. **According to him,** the robbers escaped in a helicopter.

- The police spoke with the witness**, according to whom** the robbers escaped in a helicopter.

7.3B Transform these simple sentence pairs into complex sentences using Type III Relative Clauses.

1. The CEO announced major changes. In response to these changes, many employees have voiced their concerns.

____

____

____

____

2. The match was postponed. On account of this postponement, fans were offered refunds or tickets to the rescheduled game.

____

____

____

____

3. The community center was named after a local hero. In honor of him, a special ceremony was organized.

4. The river flows through the town. By the side of the river, children love to play during the summer.

5. Crazy new evidence was presented at trial yesterday. In light of this evidence, the case took a completely different turn.

6. The city council passed a new environmental policy. As a result of this policy, local businesses started adopting green practices.

7. The company introduced new software. With the help of this software, productivity increased significantly.

8. The library was established centuries ago. Within the confines of the library, countless rare manuscripts are preserved.

9. The researchers gained access to unique data. By virtue of this data, they were able to draw groundbreaking conclusions.

10. The team had to work without their lead analyst. In the absence of the lead analyst, they faced significant challenges in completing the project.

7.4 Relative Clause Type #4: Quantity/Aspect + of Which/ Whom

These types of clauses are used when describing a part of a whole.

You can start a relative clause with any ***quantity word***:

1. I ordered five shirts. ***Two of them*** were the wrong size.

- I ordered five shirts, ***two* of which** were the wrong size.
    - » The quantity word can also go after *which/whom*. In many cases, however, it sounds awkward to put the quantity word after *which*, so use your ears. Remember, you won't go wrong if you put the quantity word at the start of the relative clause.
        - » I ordered five shirts, **of which *two*** were the wrong size.

2. Early this year, we set many goals for ourselves. We accomplished ***most* of them**.

- Early this year, we set many goals for ourselves, ***most* of which we accomplished**.
- Early this year, we set many goals for ourselves, **of which we accomplished *most***.

3. Customers ordered 1000 items. **25% of them** were returned due to defects.

- Customers ordered 1000 items, **25% of which** were returned due to defects.
- Customers ordered 1000 items, **of which 25%** were returned due to defects.

When describing people, use *whom*

1. Because of this glitch, we've gotten lots of calls from angry customers. **Many of them** have threatened to cancel their service.

- Because of this glitch, we've gotten lots of calls from angry customers, **many of whom** have threatened to cancel their service.

2. We invited 50 guests. **10 of them** couldn't make it.

- We invited 50 guests, **10 of whom** couldn't make it.

> You can use any word that represents a quantity to describe a part of a larger group:

- ..., all of which...
- ..., some of which...
- ..., most of which...
- ..., none of which...
- ..., half of which...
- ..., two-thirds of which...
- ..., all of which...
- ..., 50% of which...
- ..., much of which...
- ..., some of which...
- ..., several of which...
- ..., the vast majority of which...
- ..., none of which...

These are also common expressions:

- ..., the extent to which...
- ..., the consequence of which...
- ..., the effects of which...

Steve and I first met nearly 30 years ago, and have been colleagues, competitors and friends over the course of more than half our lives. The world rarely sees someone who has had the profound impact Steve has had, ***the effects of which*** *will be felt for many generations to come. For those of us lucky enough to get to work with him, it's been an insanely great honor. I will miss Steve immensely.*

- Bill Gates, founder of Microsoft, describing his association with Steve Jobs, founder of Apple

More examples of aspects of a whole:

The protestor threw a bucket of oil at the painting. **The surface of the painting** was fortunately protected by glass.

- The protestor threw a bucket of oil at the painting, **the surface of which** was fortunately protected by glass.

They've presented a few solutions to the problem. **None of the solutions** are realistic.

- They've presented a few solutions to the problem, **none of which** are realistic.

A significant expense for many businesses is fuel. **The cost of fuel** has been rising every year.

- A significant expense for many businesses is fuel, **the cost of which** has been rising every year.

7.4A Transform these simple sentence pairs into complex sentences using Type IV Relative Clauses.

1. The bakery sold 100 specialty cupcakes in an hour. A quarter of them were chocolate flavored.

____

____

____

2. The library acquired 300 new books last month. Half of them are on science and technology.

____

____

____

3. Our class has 25 students. Four of them have birthdays in July.

4. The zoo trip was exciting for the 30 children. Most of them saw a lion for the first time.

5. The survey received responses from 200 participants. Nearly 60% of them expressed satisfaction with the service.

6. They planned an expensive school field trip. The cost of the trip was covered by a bake sale fundraiser.

7. The unexpected freeze lasted for weeks. The effects were damaged crops.

8. They discovered an ancient artifact. The surface was inscribed with unknown symbols.

____

____

____

9. The company implemented a new policy. The consequence was a significant increase in employee productivity.

____

____

____

10. The magician performed a trick. He promised to reveal the secret at the end of the show.

____

____

____

7.5 Preposition + Possessive Pronoun

You will encounter situations where a preposition phrase is followed by the possessive relative pronoun ***whose*** (seen in Type II Relative Clauses).

This form is perfect for thanking people. It's used formulaically:

I'd like to thank/congratulate/acknowledge [SOMEONE], without whose + help/support/guidance/assistance + [THIS THING] + would have been + [ADJECTIVE RELATED TO DIFFICULTY].

In the following examples, notice that the simple sentences have **possessive pronouns**.

1. I'd like to thank our wonderful president. **Thanks to <u>her</u> leadership,** we were able to exceed all of our targets.

- I'd like to thank our wonderful president**, thanks to *<u>whose</u>*** leadership we were able to exceed all of our targets.

2. I'd like to thank my supervisor. W**ithout <u>her</u>** guidance, this project would have been impossible.

- I'd like to thank my supervisor, **without *<u>whose</u>*** guidance this project would have been impossible.

3. I'd like to thank my parents. **Without <u>their</u>** support, I couldn't have achieved my goals.

- I'd like to thank my parents, **without *<u>whose</u>*** support I couldn't have achieved my goals.

7.5A Transform these simple sentence pairs into complex sentences using Type V Relative Clauses.

1. We'd like to show our appreciation for the parent council. Without their help, we couldn't have bought this new sports equipment.

____

____

____

____

2. I'd like to congratulate the team. Without their commitment to practice, this victory would never have happened.

____

____

____

____

3. The team was led by Dr. Mars. Under his guidance, they achieved remarkable success.

4. We need to fire the company president. As a result of her errors, we now face bankruptcy.

5. We owe a lot to the librarian. Without her creativity, we wouldn't have had such engaging events.

7.6 Misplaced Modifiers

In grammar, a modifier is any word, phrase, or clause that modifies something else:

- Adjective
- Adverb
- Preposition phrase
- Relative clause
- Subordinate clause

In terms of placement, some modifiers are flexible and can be placed in different spots in a sentence, but others must go directly next to the idea they are modifying - you can't put them anywhere else.

Example: The store is on the second floor **<u>that sells children's shoes</u>**.

- <u>that sells children's shoes</u> is a misplaced modifier because it's related to "the store," not "the second floor"
- Correct version: The store **<u>that sells children's shoes</u>** is on the second floor.

7.6A Each example contains a misplaced modifier. Identify it and move it to a better spot in the sentence.

Level 1

1. Some animals are specially adapted to cold weather, like polar bears and arctic wolves.

____

____

____

____

2. Many sports involve physical contact such as hockey and football.

____

____

____

____

3. Endangered animals are killed for money, such as rhinos and elephants.

4. The goal was set by the legendary king, of bringing peace to the entire kingdom.

Level 2

1. She used to play computer games after she finished her homework for hours.

2. Different pharaohs had visions for developing Egypt, such as Akhenaton, Queen Hatshepsut, and Ramses II.

3. Great art cannot be imitated easily, like Rembrandt's or Titian's.

4. Sitting in front of the screen the whole day has become a trend among teenagers in the last few years to play and talk with peers instead of going outdoors.

Level 3

1. In the US, most people are not fit, which has an obesity rate of 36.2%.

2. Only a few species like sandfish can survive in dunes, which are a type of lizard that can swim through the smooth sand.

3. Another ride at the amusement park was also fast, but this time it made you rise into the air which I think was called The Umbrella.

4. Plastic waste is definitely the main factor behind the devastation of our oceans and land, which is discarded by thoughtless people.

8. Colon Sentences

Colons are for introducing lists, instructions, explanations, and examples (like this sentence):

1. Please buy three things for me at the grocery store: cake, chocolates, and chips.
2. I need a few more ingredients to complete my recipe: a cup of sugar, a pinch of salt, and a tablespoon of butter.
3. A problem came up when you were gone: The X501 broke down again and the technician suggested that because the machine is old, it needs to be replaced.

Capitalization after a colon:

1. Do not capitalize simple list items unless they are proper nouns.
   » Please buy three things for me at the grocery store: cake, chocolates, and chips.

2. Do not capitalize list items that are phrases.
   » I need a few more ingredients to complete my recipe: a cup of sugar, a pinch of salt, and a tablespoon of butter.
3. If the item after the colon is a complete sentence, capitalize it.
   » A problem came up when you were gone: The X501 broke down again and needs to be replaced.

9. Participial Phrases

Participial phrases can be thought of as compressed independent clauses, subordinate clauses, or relative clauses.

Participial phrases are considered a more advanced grammatical structure than subordinate and relative clauses because they are more economical (they are shorter) and flexible (they can be placed in more locations than a relative clause).

They are not called clauses because they don't have a subject or a verb.

1. Participial phrases start with participles. We'll cover the 2 most common forms:

- **Active voice** participial phrases, the most common, start with _ing words called active participles (dropping, walking)
- **Passive voice** participial phrases start with passive participles, which look like the 3rd form of the verb (give, gave, **given**; steal, stole, **stolen**).

Participles = active/passive adjectives:

Participial phrases start with a participle, which is an adjective that is conjugated for active or passive voice.

Many adjectives do not have active/passive versions: big, black, strange.

However, many adjectives have active/passive forms:

- exciting/excited
  » the exciting performer
  » the excited crowd

- boring/bored
  - » the boring teacher
  - » the bored students
- confusing/confused
  - » a confusing explanation
  - » a confused listener

Source of experience vs the one having an experience:

In these examples, the performer, the teacher, and the explanation are the source of the feeling/experience.

The crowd, the students, and the listener are the ones having the experience; they are not its source. In other words, they are the passive recipients.

2. Participial phrases can be thought of as compressed independent, subordinate, or relative clauses:

1. Independent clause > Participial phrase

Independent clause • **Active voice verb**	Sales fell. They **dropped** from 10,000 to 8000 units per month.
Participial phrase • **Active voice participle**	Sales fell, **dropping** from 10,000 to 8000 units per month.

2. Subordinate clause > Participial phrase

Subordinate clause • **Passive voice verb**	Because he **was given** a 2nd chance, he did better on the exam.
Participial phrase • **Passive voice participle**	**Given** a 2nd chance, he did better on the exam.

3. Relative clause > Participial phrase

Relative clause • **Passive voice verb**	We ate dinner, which **was followed** by dessert.
Participial phrase • **Passive voice participle**	We ate dinner, **followed** by dessert.

3. Participial phrases do not have time information.

A participle is an active voice/passive voice adjective.

Many texts refer to present participial phrases and past participial phrases. However, this text refers to active voice participial phrases and passive voice participial phrases because the participial phrase does not convey time information - it does not have a verb.

The time information is conveyed through the conjugated verb in the independent clause, not in the participial phrase. This is what also makes the grammar of participial phrases easy to remember - they don't change regardless of the tense of the rest of the sentence.

The time information is carried by the independent clause, which has the **main verb**. Whether the context is past, present, or future time, the participial phrase construction is identical:

Participial phrase • Does NOT change based on time information	Independent clause • Only the time information in the independent clause changes.	
Walking through the woods,	we **saw** deer.	**Past verb** in the independent clause
Walking through the woods,	we **see** deer all the time.	**Present verb** in the independent clause
Walking through the woods,	we **will** probably **see** deer.	**Future verb** in the independent clause

4. Participial Phrase Placement

Participial phrases are more flexible than relative clauses. Relative clauses must go directly after the idea they are related to; participial phrases can often be placed in more than one spot in a sentence.

Relative clause:

- The patient**, who was badly injured,** was brought to the clinic.
- The **relative clause** can't be placed anywhere else in this sentence.

Participial phrase:

- **Badly injured,** the patient was brought to the clinic.
- The patient, **badly injured,** was brought to the clinic.
- The patient was brought**, badly injured,** to the clinic.
- The patient was brought to the clinic **badly injured**.

5. Transformation Process

A participial phrase can be thought of as a transformation of an independent, subordinate, or relative clause:

> A. Independent clause > participial phrase transformation process

1. **Delete the subject.**
2. **Delete any auxiliary verbs.**
3. **Transform the verb into its participle.**

1. The fox jumped up. <u>He tried to reach the grapes</u> that were hanging from the tree.

1. Delete the subject *He*.
2. There is no auxiliary verb.
3. Since the verb *tried* is in active voice, transform the verb into its active participle (the _*ing* version of the word).

- **The fox jumped up <u>trying to reach the grapes</u> that were hanging from the tree.**

2. Option B was a close second. It was chosen by 2535 individuals.

1. Delete the subject *It*.
2. Delete the auxiliary verb *was*.
3. Since the verb chosen is in passive voice, transform the verb into its passive participle (no changes are needed).

- **Option B was a close second, chosen by 2535 individuals.**

B. Subordinate clause > participial phrase transformation process

1. **Delete the subordinating conjunction. We can leave some conjunctions (e.g., while, after, before).**
2. **Delete the subject.**
3. **Delete any auxiliaries.**
4. **Transform the verb into its active/passive participle.**

1. Because the fox failed to reach the grapes, he disparaged them and said, "What does it matter? They must be sour."

1. Delete the subordinating conjunction *Because*.
2. Delete the subject *the fox*.
3. There is no auxiliary verb.
4. Transform the active voice verb into its active participle.

- **Failing to reach the grapes, the fox disparaged them and said, "What does it matter? They must be sour."**

2. Because he was given a 2nd chance, he did better on the exam.

1. Delete the subordinating conjunction *Because*.
2. Delete the subject *he*.
3. Delete the auxiliary *was*.
4. Transform the passive verb into its passive participle (no changes are needed).

- **Given a 2nd chance, he did better on the exam.**

C. Relative clause > participial phrase transformation process

1. **Delete the relative pronoun.**
2. **Delete any auxiliaries.**
3. **Transform the verb into its participle.**

1. The fox jumped up. He tried to reach the grapes <u>that were hanging from the tree</u>.

   1. Delete the relative pronoun *that*.
   2. Delete the auxiliary *were*.
   3. Transform the verb into its participle (no changes are needed in this case).

- **The fox jumped up. He tried to reach the grapes <u>hanging from the tree</u>.**

D. Multiple clauses

1. The fox jumped up. He tried to reach the grapes that were hanging from the tree.

- **The fox jumped up <u>trying to reach the grapes</u> <u>hanging from the tree</u>.**
- **<u>Jumping up</u>, the fox tried to reach the grapes <u>hanging from the tree</u>.**

9.1 Active Voice Participial Phrases

"Gentlemen, we are going to relentlessly chase perfection, **knowing** full well we will not catch it."

- Vince Lombardi, legendary football coach

The *-ing* form is the most common type of participial phrase. During the transformation, regardless of the tense of the original verb, the *-ing* participle replaces the verb, any auxiliaries, and the subject. In some cases, we leave the subordinating conjunction but in others, we remove it.

Let's turn Lombardi's original statement into the subordinate clause form:

Participial phrase	Gentlemen, we are going to relentlessly chase perfection, **knowing full well we will not catch it**.
Subordinate clause	Gentlemen, we are going to relentlessly chase perfection, **even though we know full well we will not catch it**.

In the examples below, note that only the *verb in the independent clause* is conjugated for time. The participial phrase is identical regardless of the time information in the independent clause.

	Modifier	Independent Clause
Subordinate clause	After he ***got*** a raise,	he ***bought*** himself a new car.
Participial phrase	After ***getting*** a raise,	he ***bought*** himself a new car.

	Modifier	Independent Clause
Subordinate clause	After he ***gets*** a raise,	he ***will buy*** himself a new car.
Participial phrase	After ***getting*** a raise,	he ***will buy*** himself a new car.

Formula: After he got a raise/After he gets a raise > After getting a raise

1. Remove the subject *he*.
2. Remove any auxiliaries (none in these cases).
3. Change the verb to an active participle: just add *ing* to the verb with NO auxiliary (helper) verbs.

Despite the fact that... > Despite x _ing...

1. Despite the fact that X has several benefits, it's not as effective as Y.

- **Despite X having** several benefits, it's not as effective as Y.
- **Despite having** several benefits, **X is** not as effective as Y.

2. Despite the fact that X is a good product, it's not appropriate in this situation.

- **Despite X being** a good product, it's not appropriate in this situation.
- **Despite being** a good product, **X is** not appropriate in this situation.

Dummy subject participial phrases: Despite the fact that there are…

There is/There are is a common dummy subject construction: *There* doesn't actually mean anything.

Despite the fact that there are a couple minor benefits to social media for young teens, it's a poor idea overall.

- **Despite there being** a couple minor benefits to social media for young teens, it's a poor idea overall.

9.1A Transform these simple and complex sentences into sentences with participial phrases.

1. The scientist made a discovery. It changed our understanding of the world.

2. Since she practiced piano every day, she became an exceptional player.

3. He wrote a well-researched essay that impressed all his teachers.

4. After they finally completed the project, they felt a sense of accomplishment.

5. Lightning struck the old oak tree. It caused a large branch to fall.

6. The artist who's painting the mural is famous in the community.

7. The dog barked loudly. It alerted the neighbors.

8. While she was reading the novel, she discovered a hidden message.

9. The students who completed the extra credit assignments raised their grades significantly.

10. The volcano erupted last night. It spewed lava and ash over the village.

11. The musician who played the violin captivated the audience.

12. Despite the fact that group projects can foster teamwork, they're often unproductive.

____

____

____

____

9.2 Passive Voice Participial Phrases

When verbs are in passive voice, transform the clause into a passive participial phrase. It doesn't matter whether the verb is in past perfect passive voice, present simple passive voice, or past simple passive voice –the passive participial phrase looks exactly the same.

1. She spotted her bike. It had been stolen two months earlier.

1. Get rid of the subject *It*.
2. Get rid of the two auxiliaries *had been*.
3. The verb is already in its 3rd form.
    - » **She spotted her bike, stolen two months earlier.**

2. If he is given a 2nd chance to write the test, he'll do better.

1. Get rid of the subject *he*.
2. Get rid of the auxiliary *is*.
3. Get rid of the conjunction *if*.
4. The verb is already in its 3rd form.
    - » **Given a 2nd chance to write the test, he'll do better.**

3. He was attacked by a gang. He fought bravely but lost.

1. Get rid of the subject *He*.
2. Get rid of the auxiliary *was*.
3. The verb is already in its 3rd form.
    - » **Attacked by a gang, he fought bravely but lost.**

Given & Considering

Considering the circumstances is an active voice participial phrase. It means exactly the same as *given the circumstances*, which is a passive voice participial phrase.

- **Considering** the circumstances, I think this is the best choice for my needs.
- **Given** the circumstances, I think this is the best choice for my needs.
- **Considering** how high their prices are, you'd think their quality would be the best, but it's not.
- **Given** how high their prices are, you'd think their quality would be the best, but it's not.

9.2A Combine these simple sentences into complex sentences with passive participial phrases.

1. He received the scholarship. It had been established by a local entrepreneur.

____

____

____

____

2. She discovered her necklace. It had been lost during the school trip.

____

____

____

____

3. The museum unveiled the painting. It had been restored carefully over the last year.

4. The shelter took in several animals. They had been rescued from abandoned homes.

5. The artifact was returned to the museum. It had been stolen by thieves.

6. The concert was cancelled. It had been scheduled for Friday night.

7. The proposal was finally accepted. It had been submitted three months ago.

____

8. The team won the championship. They had been considered underdogs all season.

9. The building was evacuated safely. It had been threatened by the approaching storm.

10. The documentary was aired on national television. It had been produced by local students.

11. The athlete was awarded the gold medal. He had been disqualified in the previous competition.

____

____

____

____

12. The painting was sold at auction for millions of dollars. It had been considered hideous by art critics.

____

____

____

____

9.3 Participial Phrases Starting with After, Before, While, and With

If the original sentence starts with *after, before, despite,* or *while* and is in passive voice, use *being* + the 3rd form of the verb.

Get rid of the subject and any verb auxiliaries but keep the preposition/ conjunction.

1. After he was attacked by wolves, Sam never went into the forest again.

- **After being attacked** by wolves, Sam never went into the forest again.

2. Before he was admitted into the organization, he had to pass a rigourous screening.

- **Before being admitted** into the organization, he had to pass a rigorous screening.

3. While the prisoner was being transported, she escaped.

- **While being transported**, the prisoner escaped.

Despite the fact that it is/was + passive verb > Despite being + 3rd form

The participial phrase is identical regardless of the time information in the original clause:

1. Despite the fact that X **is** commonly **used** today, it's not ideal in this situation.

- **Despite X being** commonly **used** today, it's not ideal in this situation.
- **Despite being** commonly **used** today, **X** is not ideal in this situation.

2. Despite the fact that X **was** extensively **used** in the past,it's no longer used today.

- Despite **X being** extensively **used** in the past, it's no longer used today.
- Despite **being** extensively **used** in the past, **X** is no longer used today.

9.3A Combine these simple sentences into complex sentences with passive participial phrases that begin with after, before, while, and despite.

In these examples, the subordinate clause has the specific subject. In the participial phrase versions, the subject is specific in the independent clause.

1. Before the video game was released by the developers, it was beta-tested by gamers around the world.

____

____

____

____

2. After the novel was read by the book club, it was discussed in a lively meeting.

____

____

____

____

3. Before he was sent on the trip, he was given secret instructions.

4. After the essay was reviewed by the teacher, it was returned with suggestions for improvement.

5. After the recipe was perfected by the chef, it was added to the restaurant's menu.

6. While he was being arrested, the suspect bit the police officer.

7. Before he was elected prime minister, Justin Trudeau was a drama teacher.

8. Despite the fact that plastic bags are commonly used today, they're not ideal for environmental sustainability.

Participial Phrases Starting with *With*

Independent clauses	Consumers spent $383 billion on mobile phones in 2016. **36% of this spending** went to Apple and 64% of it went to other brands.
Participial phrase	Consumers spent $383 billion on mobile phones in 2016, **with 36% going** to Apple and 64% (going) to other brands.

Independent clauses	About 80% of students said that mostly their female friends are called out for dress code violations. **Only 3.7% of students witnessed** a boy being called out for dress code violations.
With + noun + participle	About 80% of students said that mostly their female friends are called out for dress code violations, **with only 3.7% of students witnessing** a boy being called out for dress code violations.

Transformations of Noun Clauses (+ Independent Clause)

I agree that > I agree with

- I agree/disagree **that a dress code should be implemented** at our school.
- I agree/disagree **with a dress code being implemented** at our school.

Transformations of If Clauses (*If* + Independent Clause)

I'm fine if > I'm fine with

- I'm fine **if this is done** tomorrow.
- I'm fine **with this being done** tomorrow.

I'm not ok if > I'm not ok with

- **I'm not okay if this is done** tomorrow. It needs to be done today!
- **I'm not okay with this being done** tomorrow. It needs to be done today!

9.3C Combine these simple sentences into complex sentences with participial phrases starting with ***with.***

1. The city allocated $5 million to public park improvements last year. $2 million of this budget was used for playground upgrades and the rest for landscaping.

____

____

____

____

2. In the survey, 90% of participants expressed concern about climate change. However, only 50% reported changing their daily habits to reduce their carbon footprint.

____

____

____

____

3. I'm comfortable if the team starts the project without me.

4. The school announced a new online learning platform this semester. 70% of the feedback from students and parents has been positive.

5. Nearly 60% of the workforce has transitioned to remote work. Only 10% report a preference for the office environment.

6. The committee approved the budget for the next fiscal year. However, some members expressed concerns about the allocation for health services.

7. The new software update was released last night. Many users are reporting issues with installation.

8. I'm disappointed because the project is delayed again.

9. The company achieved a 15% increase in sales this quarter. This success is largely attributed to the new marketing campaign.

9.4 Perfect Active Voice Participial Phrases

Perfect active voice participial phrases deal with experience, like present perfect.

	Modifier	Independent Clause
Subordinate clause with present perfect verb	Because I**'ve been** to Paris,	I can tell you about all the places that are worth visiting.
Participial phrase	**Having been** to Paris,	I can tell you about all the places that are worth visiting.

	Modifier	Independent Clause
Subordinate clause with present perfect verb	Because I **haven't been** to Paris,	I can't tell you what's worth visiting there.
Participial phrase	**Not having been** to Paris,	I can't tell you what's worth visiting there.

Present Simple vs. Present Perfect Transformations

	Modifier	Independent Clause
Independent clause with present simple verb	I **have** kids.	I don't get as much sleep as I'd like to get.
Participial phrase	**Having** kids,	I don't get as much sleep as I'd like to get.

VS.

	Modifier	Independent Clause
Independent clause with present perfect verb	I **have had** kids too.	I know what it's like to not get much sleep.
Participial phrase	**Having had** kids too,	I know what it's like to not get much sleep.

Formula:

If the original verb is in present perfect (I have studied) or past perfect (I had studied), the participial phrase is *having* + the 3rd form (give, gave, **given**).

Present Perfect

In the example transformations below, all the verbs in the first simple sentence are in **present perfect**. All the participial phrases are in perfect active voice.

1. Usain Bolt **has broken** the record. He is now famous around the world.

- **Having broken** the record, Bolt is now famous around the world.
- Bolt, **having broken** the record, is now famous around the world.

2. **I have studied** the company's policies and procedure. I am confident I'm ready for the job.

- **Having studied** the company's policies and procedures, I am confident I'm ready for the job.

3. **I have tried** different ways of cooking pumpkin. I think the recipe which my neighbour gave me last week is the best.

- **Having tried** different ways of cooking pumpkin, I think the recipe which my neighbour gave me last week is the best.

Past Perfect

In the example transformations below, all the verbs in the first simple sentence are in **past perfect**. All the participial phrases are in perfect active voice.

1. **I had had** no experience in the field. I took the job anyway because I knew I could do it.

- **Having had** no experience in the field, I took the job anyway because I knew I could do it.

2. **She had worked** at several companies in this field. She shared a lot of good business practices.

- **Having worked** at several companies in this field, she shared a lot of good business practices.

3. **He had never** seen such a case before. He consulted his colleagues.

- **Having never seen** such a case before, he consulted his colleagues.
- **Never having seen** such a case before, he consulted his colleagues.

9.4A Combine these simple sentences into complex sentences with perfect participial phrases.

1. Because I've read the entire book series, I can discuss all the plot twists and character developments.

2. Because I haven't finished my homework, I can't go out with my friends tonight.

3. I have listened to this musician many times. I'm familiar with his work.

4. Serena Williams has won multiple Grand Slam titles. She is considered one of the greatest tennis players of all time.

5. I have researched the topic extensively. I am prepared to lead the discussion in tomorrow's meeting.

____

____

____

____

6. I haven't visited the new museum exhibit yet. I can't give you a personal opinion about it.

____

____

____

____

7. The team had lost three games in a row. They practiced even harder to break the losing streak.

____

____

____

____

8. She had studied abroad in Japan for a year. She brought back unique perspectives to her studies.

____

____

____

____

9. They had completed the marathon despite the bad weather. They felt a tremendous sense of achievement.

10. I had researched the topic for months. I was ready to present my findings at the conference.

11. He had never traveled outside of his home country. He was thrilled about his upcoming trip.

12. We had watched all the tutorials available. We started creating our own videos.

9.5 Perfect Passive Participial Phrases

Perfect passive participial phrases deal with experiences or events that happened in the past and are relevant now. This structure can be used to transform present perfect passive and past simple passive into perfect participial phrases.

Present perfect passive verb	The president **has been briefed** on the latest developments. He is ready to give a press conference.
Perfect passive participial phrase	**Having been briefed on the latest developments**, the president is ready to give a press conference.

9.5A Combine these simple sentences into complex sentences with perfect passive participial phrases.

1. The new policies have been approved by the government. They will be implemented starting next month.

____

____

____

____

2. The software has been updated by the development team. It now includes new security features.

____

____

____

____

3. The lost kitten has been found by the neighborhood kids. It's safe at home now.

4. The science fair projects have been evaluated by the teachers. The best projects will go to the regional competition.

5. The player has been accused of doping, so he is suspended pending drug tests.

6. We have been given the day off, so we are going for a long bike ride.

7. She was made redundant. She had to start looking for a new job.

____

____

____

____

8. The novel has been translated into thirty languages. It is now accessible worldwide.

____

____

____

____

9. The old mansion has been renovated by the city. It serves as a museum now.

____

____

____

____

10. The documentary has been viewed by millions. It sparked a global conversation on this controversial topic.

____

____

____

____

10. Noun Clauses

A noun clause is a large noun, one that has a subject and a predicate. Noun clauses start with the W5H words and *that*:

who	Do you know**who that is**? I don't know **who ate your cookie**.
what	I don't know**what he said**.
where	We have to change **where we are going to hold the party**. On the form, you must indicate **where you were born**.
when	Have you decided **when the meeting will take place**? I don't know **when she's arriving**.
why	I don't know**why he did that**. I don't know **why I'm here**.
how	I don't know**how he did that**. I'd like to know **how to do this correctly**.
whoever	**Whoever arrives late** will be punished.
whatever	**Whatever you say** will likely upset her.

Noun Clauses Can Also Begin with *That*

Noun clauses also begin with *that*. In these cases, *that* means *the fact that*.

- Did you know **that** the president is visiting us tomorrow?
  - » A noun clause differs from an adjective/relative clause in that it functions as a noun (subject or object) rather than as an adjective. You can tell that this is a noun clause and not a relative clause because the clause answers the question "Did you know WHAT?"
- I didn't know **that** he is a cop.
  - » I didn't know WHAT? I didn't know THAT HE IS A COP.
- I like **that** John lives next door.
  - » I'm not saying I like John. I'm saying I like the fact that John lives next door. Maybe I like to borrow his tools.

10.1A Rewrite these sentences so that each one contains a noun clause. The new sentences should have the same meaning as the originals.

Note: Multiple answers are possible.

1. Who will lead the project next month? Can you explain this to me?

Can you explain who

____

____

2. She couldn't remember her breakfast this morning.

She couldn't remember what

____

____

3. They are discussing their vacation plans. They aren't sure of a location to go to.

They are discussing where

____

____

4. He asked about my job start date.

He asked me when

____

____

5. She questioned the decision. Why was it made without her?

She questioned why

____

____

6. How did they solve the problem? Can you show me?

Can you show me how

---

7. The competition winner will receive a scholarship.

Whoever

---

8. What did he tell you? Tell me everything.

Tell me whatever

---

9. Her fluency in three languages is surprising.

It's surprising that

---

10. Do you know the owner of the notebook that was left on the table?

Do you know whose

---

11. Subjunctive Mood: Noun Clauses for Orders and Suggestions

Verbs in noun clauses with an order or suggestion require **subjunctive mood**, which makes them infinitive (the base form of the verb, which has no time information). The verb in the independent clause is conjugated normally.

	Independent Clause	Noun Clause in Subjunctive Mood
Past	The doctor suggested	*that she exercise regularly.
Present	The doctor suggests	*that she exercise regularly.
Future	The doctor will suggest	*that she exercise regularly.

***Notice:** It does NOT say ...that she exercis**es** regularly.

It doesn't matter what the tense is in the independent clause. It could be past, present, or future. In all of these cases, the order/suggestion in the **noun clause** will look EXACTLY the same: a bare infinitive ("exercise").

Negatives

Forming the negative in subjunctive mood: *not* + bare infinitive

Present

- I suggest that you **wear** that to the meeting.
- I suggest that you **not wear** that to the meeting.

Past

- His wife suggested that he **wear** that to the meeting.
- His wife suggested that he **not wear** that to the meeting.

Future

- I'll suggest that he **wear** that to the meeting.
- I'll suggest that he **not wear** that to the meeting.

Verbs that use this structure

Ask

- He asked that I see him tomorrow.
- I ask that you talk quietly in the library.
- He asked that she come tomorrow instead of today.

Demand

- My neighbour demanded that I turn down the volume.
- The client demands that the company fix the problem immediately.

Insist

- My boss insists that we all show up 10 minutes early for each shift.
- The doctor will probably insist that he avoid any strenuous exercise.

Order

- The coach ordered that he show up to practice on time.

Recommend

- I recommend that she exercise regularly.

Suggest

- I suggest that you not get this colour.
- I suggest that he avoid/not eat spicy food.

Require

- We require that all guests sign in at the door.

Request

- I have requested that he send payment immediately.

Phrases that use this structure

It is essential that...

- It's essential that we provide the highest level of customer service.

It is advised that...

- It is advised that you not go there.

It's important that...

- It's important that he be ready on time.

I would ask that...

- I would ask that nothing happen/be done while I'm away.

It is critical that...

- It's critical that he follow every step of the instructions precisely.

It is crucial that...

- It's crucial that he see me first thing tomorrow morning.

It is necessary that...

- It is necessary that he get a check-up on a monthly basis.

Some verbs can take the subject-verb-object or subjunctive mood structure

Ask

- I asked him to help me.
- I asked that he help me.

Command

- I commanded him to help me.
- I commanded that he help me.

Order

- I ordered him to help me.
- I ordered that he help me.

Require

- I required him to help me.
- I required that he help me.

Urge

- I urged him to help me.
- I urged that he help me.

Beg

- I begged him to help me.
- I begged that he help me.

ONLY subjunctive mood is correct with these verbs

Insist

- INCORRECT ~~I insisted him to help me.~~
- CORRECT I insisted that he help me.

Propose

- INCORRECT ~~I proposed him to help me.~~
- CORRECT I proposed that he help me.

Recommend

- INCORRECT ~~I recommended him to help me.~~
- CORRECT I recommended that he help me.

Request

- INCORRECT ~~I requested him to help me.~~
- CORRECT I requested that he help me.

There are several ways to use *recommend*

I recommend **the sweet and sour chicken**.

- noun phrase

I recommend **going to Disney World**.

- noun (gerund) phrase

The doctor recommended **that she exercise regularly**.

- noun clause in subjunctive mood

> 11.1A Rewrite these sentences so that each one contains subjunctive mood. The new sentences should have the same meaning as the originals.

1. You should inform him of the decision immediately.

I ask that he

____

____

____

____

2. The lawyer demanded, "release my client from custody."

The lawyer demanded that her client

3. She says, "everyone needs to arrive on time for the meeting."

She insists that everyone

4. The judge ordered the evidence to be presented by tomorrow.

The judge ordered that the evidence

5. The doctor says, "take the medication twice a day."

The doctor recommends that you

6. He said, "she should study more if she wants to pass the exam."

He suggests that she

___

___

___

___

7. The company requires all employees to undergo annual training.

The company requires that all employees

___

___

___

___

8. Please deliver this package by noon.

I request that this package

___

___

___

___

9. They advise travelers to check weather conditions before departing.

They advise that travelers

___

___

___

___

10. He said, "take a different route to avoid traffic."

He proposed that we

____

____

____

____

11. It is essential for everyone to remain calm during the drill.

It is essential that everyone

____

____

____

____

12. You are advised to save your work frequently to avoid data loss.

It is advised that you

____

____

____

____

13. Following the instructions to the letter is crucial to ensure safety.

It is crucial that the instructions

____

____

____

____

14. I would like you to keep this information confidential until the announcement.

I would ask that you

____

____

____

____

15. Acting now to prevent further damage is vital.

It is vital that we

____

____

____

____

12. Appositives & Adjective Phrases and Clusters

12.1 Appositives

Appositives are one of the simplest structures. Basically, they are synonyms. **Appositives** are just a noun, noun phrase, or noun clause and follow directly after <u>the noun they are synonymous with</u>.

- <u>My friend</u>, **John**, has arrived.
- <u>My car</u>, **an old Toyota**, is in the shop again.
- For Sweden, emissions were around 8.5 metric tons in 1980 and decreased steadily until they reached roughly <u>4.5 metric tons in 2020</u>, **a reduction of 50%**.
- Last year, our company earned <u>$1 million</u>, **an increase of 50% over 2020**.
- He deposited <u>the paycheck</u>, **a pittance for all his hard work**.

- He drives an old car, **a beat-up rust bucket**.
- He went for a drive, **a quick spin around the block**.

Apple picking is a cherished rite of fall, **a wholesome and fun family outing, a throwback to a simpler time when people weren't so disconnected from the production of their sustenance**.

- Source: Daniel Gross. "Against Apple Picking"
- Both **appositives** refer back to a cherished rite of fall.
- The first appositive (a wholesome and fun family outing) is a noun phrase.
- The second appositive is a noun phrase (a throwback to a simpler time) containing a subordinate clause (when people weren't so disconnected from the production of their sustenance).

Referring to the 2016 fires in Fort McMurray, British Columbia: The hardest thing to describe is the wind, **a deep gut punch of a blast powerful enough to form dust spirals along the highway, and nearly as hot on your face as when you open an oven**.

Source: Tim Querengesser, Metro Edmonton

Appositives vs Relative Clauses

An appositive is often a good substitute for a relative clause when the relative clause is synonymous with the noun it's related to:

My car is almost dead. It's a 2008 Corolla.

Relative clause	My car, which is a 2008 Corolla, is almost dead.
Appositive	My car**, a 2008 Corolla,** is almost dead.

He found the treasure at a garage sale. It was a masterpiece. It had been created by an unknown artist.

Relative clause	He found the treasure at a garage sale. It was a masterpiece **that had been created by an unknown artist**.
Participial phrase	He found the treasure at a garage sale. It was a masterpiece **created by an unknown artist**.
Appositive	He found the treasure, **a masterpiece created by an unknown artist,** at a garage sale.

12.1A Rewrite these sentences so that each one contains an appositive. The new sentences should have the same meaning as the originals

1. My brother, who is an engineer, works in a multinational company.

____

____

____

____

2. Leonardo da Vinci, who was a renowned painter, also excelled in engineering.

____

____

____

____

3. Mount Everest, which is the highest mountain in the world, attracts numerous climbers every year.

4. The novel "War and Peace", which is a masterpiece written by Leo Tolstoy, is considered one of the greatest books of all time.

5. Albert Einstein, who developed the theory of relativity, is one of the most famous scientists in history.

6. "The Scream", which was painted by Edvard Munch, has become an iconic symbol of existential angst.

7. Wolfgang Amadeus Mozart, who was a prolific and influential composer, left a significant mark on the history of Western music.

8. The Tesla Roadster, which is an electric sports car, can accelerate from 0 to 60 mph in just 1.9 seconds.

9. The Sphinx, which is a mythical creature with the body of a lion and the head of a human, is a symbol of ancient Egypt.

10. The Great Barrier Reef, which is the world's largest coral reef system, is home to thousands of marine species.

12.2 Adjective Clusters and Phrases

Adjective clusters, which function just like appositives, can be adjectives or adjective phrases that modify the preceding noun:

- He stared at his opponent, **huge, aggressive, and ready to fight**.

Adjective phrases can modify the entire preceding clause:

- She stormed into the teacher's office, **furious about her grades**.
- The closet was crammed to the ceiling, **full of bags and boxes**.
- [Asian students' outstanding] results apply regardless of where Asians live, ***readily*** **apparent in the percentage of Asian Americans in the country's most competitive magnet high schools and elite universities**.
    - » **NOTE:** If an ***adverb*** modifies the head adjective ("apparent"), it's still considered an adjective phrase.

Adjective phrases often begin with:

- full of..., complete with...
- angry about..., furious about...., sad about..., happy about..., delighted about...

12.2A Rewrite these sentences so that each one contains an adjective cluster or phrase. The new sentences should have the same meaning as the originals

Note: All of the sentences to be transformed into adjective phrases/clusters have a BE verb (is, was, were).

1. The cat moved silently across the garden. It was sleek and shadowy. It was alert for any sign of movement.

____

____

____

____

2. He handed in his resignation. He was firm in his decision. He was ready for a new beginning.

3. The garden was blooming. It was full of vibrant colors and the sweet scent of spring flowers.

4. The old museum finally opened its doors after a long renovation. It's rich in history and alive with the stories of the past.

5. The old library book held secrets of the past. It was worn and fragile.

6. Her new song played on the radio everywhere for months. It was catchy and uplifting.

7. The puppy raced across the yard. It was small, fluffy, and energetic. It was eager to play with anyone who would give it attention.

8. She finished her painting. She was proud of her work. However, she was anxious about displaying it at the school art show.

9. The children were ready to dive into the latest story. They were full of anticipation.

10. The undefeated basketball team entered the gym. They were confident in their ability to win the championship.

13. Nominative Absolutes

Nominative absolutes are freestanding descriptions, often related to the entire main clause.

- [The cat] was sitting as still as a statue, **its eyes fixed unblinkingly on the far corner of Privet Drive**. (J.K. Rowling. Harry Potter and the Philosopher's Stone)

NOTE 1: As grammar structures get more advanced, they get simpler. The nominative absolute, compared to the subordinate clause, doesn't have a verb or subordinating conjunction. In fact, absolute nominatives don't start with any conjunction.

NOTE 2: In some cases, you might need to add the preposition *with*. Use your ears.

NOTE 3: Don't overuse these. Good writing uses a wide variety of sentence structures. No writer thinks "I really want to use a nominative absolute in this sentence."

13.1 Subject Complement to Nominative Absolute Transformation

Note that the following independent clauses that are transformed into nominative absolutes have a BE verb followed by an adjective phrase (this is a subject complement).

Transformation rules:

- Keep the subject.
- Delete the *be* verb.

1. The monster could barely move. Its belly **was** full of children.
   » The monster could barely move, its belly full of children.
2. The criminals sat around the table planning. Their minds **were** full of schemes.
   » The criminals sat around the table planning, their minds full of schemes.
3. The soldiers were ambushed. Their guard **was** down in the supposedly safe part of town.
   » The soldiers were ambushed, their guard down in the supposedly safe part of town.
4. He slept in his seat. His bag **was** directly above him in the luggage rack.
   » He slept in his seat, his bag directly above him in the luggage rack.
5. He gazed in wonder at the skyscrapers. The buildings **were** as tall as mountains.
   » He gazed in wonder at the skyscrapers, buildings as tall as mountains.
6. The teacher inspired her students. Her passion for education **was** evident in every lesson.
   » The teacher inspired her students, her passion for education evident in every lesson.

In some cases, we add "with" to the beginning of the nominative absolute. You will need to trust your ears.

As in the previous section, note that all the subordinate clauses below have a BE verb followed by a subject complement. "Went" in the final sentence means "became/was."

1. **When the fighting was over,** the soldiers rejoiced.
    - **The fighting over,** the soldiers rejoiced.
    - **With the fighting over,** the soldiers rejoiced.
2. **After the exam was over**, the weary students trudged home.
    - **The exam over**, the weary students trudged home.
    - **With the exam over**, the weary students trudged home.
3. **After their company went bankrupt**, the two partners started from scratch.
    - **Their company bankrupt**, the two partners started from scratch.
    - **With their company bankrupt**, the two partners started from scratch.

13.1A Combine these sentences by transforming one of them into a nominative absolute.

1. The city arose from the desert. The gleaming towers were a sign of economic progress.

____

____

____

____

2. She glared at him in silence. The only sound was the ticking clock.

____

____

____

____

3. She listened intently to the music. The notes were as sweet as honey.

4. They admired the painting. Its colours were as vibrant as a rainbow.

5. He watched the waves crash against the shore. The sound was as soothing as a lullaby.

6. He went for a walk. A hat was on his head to protect him against the sun.

7. The security guard stood there impassively. His uniform was crisp and clean.

8. The concert was over. The crowd filed out of the arena.

9. The game was won. The team celebrated with high-fives and cheers.

13.2 Noun/Possessive Noun + Active Participial Phrase

These examples do not use a BE verb in the original version. This transformation pattern looks like a noun or possessive noun followed by an active voice participial phrase.

In some cases, *with* is appropriate at the start of the nominative absolute. Again, trust your ears.

Transformation rules:

- Remove any conjunction.
- Keep the subject.
- Transform the full active voice verb into an active participle.

1. We walked on the beach. The sand shifted beneath our toes.
   » We walked on the beach, **the sand shifting** beneath our toes.
2. He rode off in the old junker. Its exhaust spewed clouds of black smoke.
   » He rode off in the old junker, **its exhaust spewing** clouds of black smoke.
3. She sped off on her electric scooter. Her hair was blowing in the wind.
   » She sped off on her electric scooter, **her hair blowing** in the wind.
4. Samsung saw a massive decline in China in 2015 **as its smart phone market share dropped by half** in 12 months.
   » Samsung saw a massive decline in China in 2015, (with) **its smart phone market share dropping by half** in 12 months.

13.2A Combine these sentences by transforming one of them into a nominative absolute.

1. We hiked through the forest. The leaves rustled beneath our feet.

____

____

____

____

2. They floated down the river. The water gently carried them along.

____

____

____

____

3. He marched down the street. His boots clunked on the pavement.

4. She skated across the rink. Her blades glided smoothly over the ice.

5. She drove away in the sports car. The engine roared as she shifted gears.

6. The chef prepared a delectable dish. Its aroma filled the entire restaurant.

7. We trekked up the mountain. The rocks shifted and slid beneath our boots.

8. We strolled through the park. The autumn leaves crunched under our shoes.

9. The singer performed a powerful ballad. Her voice resonated through the concert hall.

13.3 Noun/Possessive Noun + Passive Participial Phrase

Transformation rules:

- Remove any conjunction.
- Keep the subject.
- Transform the full passive verb into a passive participle.

1. As soon as his opponent **was defeated**, the victorious boxer punched the sky and then hugged his trainer.
   » **(With) His opponent defeated**, the victorious boxer punched the sky and then hugged his trainer.
2. The security guard stood there impassively. His enormous arms **were folded** across his chest.
   » The security guard stood there impassively, **his enormous arms folded** across his chest.
3. He stood there ready to fight. His fingers **were** tightly **clenched** into fists.
   » He stood there ready to fight, **(with) his fingers tightly clenched** into fists.

13.3A Combine these sentences by transforming one of them into a passive nominative absolute.

- Note: In many cases, you can transform either sentence into a participial phrase, but for this exercise, transform the passive one.
- In a couple cases, both sides can be transformed into passive nominative absolutes, but one of the options will *sound* much better than the other.

1. The exam was completed. The students were allowed to leave the classroom.

____

____

____

____

2. The project was finished. The team celebrated with a well-deserved break.

3. The issue was resolved. The customer was pleased with the company's service.

4. The meeting was adjourned. The attendees filed out of the conference room.

5. The speech was concluded. The audience gave the speaker a standing ovation.

6. The tourists were robbed. Their wallets were stolen in the crowded market.

7. The chef was frustrated. His dish was ruined by a mistake in the recipe.

8. The recipe was laid out before her. She began mixing the ingredients to bake a delicious cake.

BONUS 14. Cumulative & Suspensive Syntax

You won't learn any new sentence structures in this section. Here we concern ourselves with the arrangement of clauses and phrases and the effects achieved by changing their order.

First, we have to be clear about a few terms:

Modifier: Any word that modifies the meaning of another word, phrase, or clause

- Adjectives, adverbs, relative clauses, subordinate clauses, preposition phrases, and participial phrases are all modifiers.

Bound modifier: A modifier that needs to go directly next to the idea it's related to

- "Bound" means "tied to something." For example, a relative clause MUST go directly after the idea it's related to. That's why it's called a "bound" modifier.

Free modifier: A modifier that doesn't need to go directly next to the idea it's related to

- A free modifier isn't restricted in the same way as a bound modifier. A free modifier can be placed in a variety of locations, so you can move it around for better cohesion or rhetorical purposes (described below).

Base clause: Independent clause

- Every sentence, no matter how short or long, needs to have an independent clause. This is the grammatical core of the sentence.

Two General Methods of Adding Modifiers: Cumulative and Suspensive Style

The techniques described in this section are frequently seen in fiction but rarely employed deliberately in academic writing.

Cumulative Syntax = Accumulation of Details

- When the **base clause** is at the beginning of the sentence, or toward the beginning, this is known as cumulative syntax because the modifiers accumulate details after the base clause.
- **He climbed the mountain** through the driving snow, indifferent to the wind and the cold.

Suspensive Syntax = Delayed Revelation of Ideas

- When the **base clause** is at the end of the sentence, this is known as suspensive syntax because the reader must get to the end of the sentence (where the base clause is) before they get to the point of the sentence. This technique is often used to create suspense.
- Through the driving snow, indifferent to the wind and the cold, **he climbed the mountain**.

Levels of Modification

Modifiers can modify either the base clause or other modifiers. This is referred to as levels of modification:

- **Level one:** the base clause (only the base clause by itself is a complete sentence)
- **Level two:** a modifier of the base clause
- **Level three:** a modifier of the level two modifier
- **Level four:** a modifier of the level three modifier

I remember him *as if it were yesterday, as he came plodding to the inn door, his sea-chest following behind him in a hand-barrow – a tall, strong, heavy, nut-brown man, his tarry pigtail falling over the shoulder of his soiled blue coat, his hands ragged and scarred, with black, broken nails, and the sabre cut across one cheek, a dirty, livid white.*

- Robert Louis Stevenson. *Treasure Island*
- **Base clause**

Level 1	Level 2	Level 3	Level 4
I remember him	as if it were yesterday,		
	as he came plodding to the inn door,	his sea-chest following behind him in a hand-barrow	
	– a tall, strong, heavy, nut-brown man,	his tarry pigtail falling over the shoulder of his soiled blue coat,	
		his hands ragged and scarred,	with black, broken nails,
		and the sabre cut across one cheek,	a dirty, livid white.

Level 1	I remember him	← All L2 modifiers refer back to the L1 base clause
Level 2	as if it were yesterday	
Level 2	as he came plodding to the inn door	
Level 3	his sea-chest following behind him in a hand-barrow	
Level 2	a tall, strong, heavy, nut-brown man,	← These L3 modifiers refer back to "a tall man"
Level 3	his tarry pigtail falling over the shoulder of his soiled blue coat,	
Level 3	his hands ragged and scarred	← This L4 modifier refer back to "his hands" (L3)
Level 4	with black, broken nails,	
Level 3	and the sabre cut across one cheek,	← This L4 modifier refer back to "the sabre cut"
Level 4	a dirty, livid white.	

Example of a 7-**level pattern**. Most modifiers refer to the preceding modifier:

The earliest known evidence of the cultivation of fire goes back to a period as remote from that of Neanderthal man as is his dim day from our own, namely, that of Pithecanthropus, some 500,000 years ago, in the dens of the ravenous low-browed cannibal known as Peking Man, who was particularly fond, apparently, of brains a la nature, gobbled raw from freshly opened skulls.

- Campbell, Joseph. *Myths to Live By*

Level 1	**The earliest known evidence of the cultivation of fire goes back to a period**
Level 2	as remote from that of Neanderthal man as is his dim day from our own (a general description of the time period)
Level 3	namely, that of Pithecanthropus (the specific name of the hominid)
Level 4	some 500,000 years ago, (the specific date)
Level 4	in the dens of the ravenous low-browed cannibal (location)
Level 5	known as Peking Man, (specific name)
Level 6	who was particularly fond, apparently, of brains *a la nature*, (behaviour)
Level 7	gobbled raw from freshly opened skulls. (detail about behaviour)

14.1A Combine these sentences according to the guidance.

We were hiking through the forest.

This was in the autumn.

We saw a deer.

It was an enormous male whitetail.

He was ready for the winter in his thick, grey coat.

He was completely unafraid of our presence.

His enormous antlers were a sign of his strength.

- Transform the 1st sentence into a participial phrase.
- Transform the 2nd sentence into a preposition phrase.
- **The 3rd sentence will be the independent clause.**
- Transform the 4th sentence into an appositive.
- Transform the 5th and 6th sentences into adjective phrases.
- Transform the 7th sentence into a nominative absolute.

1. ______________________________

____

____

____

____

____

____

____

The crowd watched.

The match began.

It was an arm wrestling competition.

It was held once a year.

It gave the winner the title of "strongest man in Latchford."

Latchford is Ontario's smallest town.

The population is 387.

- Transform the 1st sentence into a subordinate clause.
- **The 2nd sentence will be the independent clause.**
- Transform the 3rd sentence into an appositive.
- Transform the 4th sentence into a passive participial phrase.
- Transform the 5th sentence into an active participial phrase.
- Transform the 6th sentence into an appositive.
- Transform the 7th sentence into a nominative absolute.

2.____

They had finally escaped the party.

It was a high school reunion.

They had not really enjoyed it.

The loud music made it impossible to communicate.

They drove and they talked.

- Transform the 1st sentence into a perfect participial phrase.
- Transform the 2nd sentence into an appositive.
- Transform the 3rd sentence into a relative clause.
- Transform the 4th sentence into a nominative absolute.
- **The 5th sentence will be the independent clause.**

3. ____

She was lost in a new city.

She had given up waiting for her friend.

She walked in the rain.

It was a drizzle.

The drizzle had been falling all day.

She was searching for a taxi.

- Transform the 1st sentence into an adjective phrase.
- Transform the 2nd sentence into a perfect participial phrase.
- **The 3rd sentence will be the independent clause.**
- Transform the 4th sentence into an appositive.
- Transform the 5th sentence into a relative clause.
- Transform the 6th sentence into a participial phrase.

4. ____

He was barely able to keep his eyes open.

He drank a cup of coffee.

The coffee was black.

It was the first of many that day.

The day would be filled with interminable meetings.

- Transform the 1st sentence into an adjective phrase.
- **The 2nd sentence will be the independent clause.**
- Transform the 3rd sentence into an adjective.
- Transform the 4th sentence into an appositive.
- Transform the 5th sentence into an appositive + relative clause.

5. ____

He stepped away from the computer.
It was a sleek machine.
It was both a blessing and the bane of his existence.
He slammed it shut.
He dropped his glasses on top of it.
His eyes were weary of searching through infinite files for the missing data.
The data was needed by his boss.
His boss was a ruthless perfectionist.
He drove his employees to the breaking point.
He was indifferent to their family lives.
He demanded total dedication to the job.

- **The 1st sentence will be the independent clause.**
- Transform the 2nd sentence into an appositive.
- Transform the 3rd sentence into a relative clause.
- Transform the 4th and 5th sentences into active participial phrases.
- Transform the 6th sentence into a nominative absolute.
- Transform the 7th sentence into a passive participial phrase.
- Transform the 8th sentence into an appositive.
- Transform the 9th sentence into a relative clause.
- Transform the 10th sentence into an adjective phrase.
- Transform the 11th sentence into an active participial phrase.

6. ____

____

____

____

____

____

____

Summary

Now that you've finished "Cracking the Code on Complex Sentences," the secrets of great writing have been fully revealed to you. You'll see these patterns everywhere you look now. Whenever you're reading a good book, you'll understand *how* the author crafted such great prose.

I especially hope this book has made a big difference in the quality of your writing and in the quality of your students' and children's writing. More importantly, I hope it has made a difference in your enjoyment of writing. People tend to like what they're good at!

Did you check out the online resources that come with this book? New resources are added regularly, and you can always request new lessons and resources for yourself or your students. These exercises will keep your skills sharp and your students engaged.

If you're looking for a writing course for your child or for your students, AEM Academy has an academic writing program for kids and teens as well as a test prep program for IELTS. If you're looking for a writing course for yourself, I have a program that helps professionals develop writing skills needed to move up to leadership roles. It's helped many of my students get promoted.

Don't be a stranger! Let me know if you need help with either your own writing skills or those of your students.

To your success,

Jan Waginski

June 22, 2024

Exercise Answers

Chapter 1

1.2A Punctuation in Independent Clauses

1. This paragraph is missing six periods. Add them.

Canada is a big country in North America. **It's** famous for its friendly people, beautiful landscapes, and cold weather. **Canada** has mountains, forests, lakes, and rivers and is home to many different animals like moose, bears, and beavers. **In** Canada, we speak two official languages: English and French. **Some** fun things to do in Canada include ice skating, skiing, going to the beach, camping, and watching hockey. **If** you ever visit Canada, make sure to try poutine, a delicious Canadian dish made of French fries, gravy, and cheese curds.

2. This paragraph is missing seven commas.

Poland is a large country in eastern Europe. It has many beautiful places to **visit,** like sandy beaches by the sea up north and big mountains down south. For outdoor **fun,** you can go hiking in the mountains or kayaking on the lakes. Poland also has many exciting **festivals, castles,** and old cities full of stories to discover. The food is good too! In **Poland,** they eat tasty things like **dumplings, sausages,** and warm stew with meat and cabbage.

1.2B Independent Clause or Fragment?

1. Are these proper independent clauses or fragments?

a)	Independent clause	**Fragment**	When a student is given a math test or a question.
b)	Independent clause	**Fragment**	The main cause of drunk driving.
c)	**Independent clause**	Fragment	I prefer staying at home.
d)	**Independent clause**	Fragment	Firstly, there is expertise.

e)	**Independent clause**	Fragment	People with a healthy lifestyle generally feel good about themselves.
f)	Independent clause	**Fragment**	If you have high blood pressure for an extended period of time.
g)	Independent clause	**Fragment**	First, the causes of waste in the ocean.
h)	Independent clause	**Fragment**	Is one of the richest and most popular YouTubers.
i)	Independent clause	**Fragment**	For example, a backpack and a hat.
j)	**Independent clause**	Fragment	It's over.

1.2C Review of Key Concepts in Simple Sentences

1. What is the technical term for a simple sentence? <u>Independent clause</u>

2. What is a clause? A clause typically consists of a/an <u>subject</u> followed by a/an <u>predicate</u>, which is made up of at least a/an <u>verb</u> and the words after it. A subject is generally a/an <u>noun</u>. So is an object.

3. Identify the SUBJECT in each sentence.

a) **A dog** had stolen a piece of meat out of a butcher's shop.

b) On his way home, **he** was crossing a river.

4. Identify the complete VERB in each sentence.

a) A dog **had stolen** a piece of meat out of a butcher's shop.

b) On his way home, he **was crossing** a river.

c) He **saw** his reflection in the stream below.

d) He **dropped** his piece of meat and so lost all.

5. Identify the PREDICATE in each sentence.

a) On his way home, he **was crossing a river.**

b) He **saw his reflection in the stream below.**

6. Identify the complete OBJECT in each sentence.

a) A dog had stolen **a piece of meat** out of a butcher's shop.

b) Hewas crossing **a river**.

c) He saw **his reflection** in the stream below.

d) Unfortunately, he dropped **his piece of meat** and so lost all.

7. Identify the ADVERB in each sentence.

a) **Greedily**, he resolved to secure the meat.

b) **Unfortunately**, he dropped his piece of meat and so lost all.

8. Identify the PREPOSITION/S in each sentence.

a) A dog had stolen a piece of meat **out of** a butcher's shop.

b) **On** his way home, he was crossing a river.

c) He mistook it **for** another dog **with** another piece of meat.

9. This fable is missing eight periods. Write them in.

The Crow and the Pitcher

A crow was nearly dead from thirst. **He** spied a pitcher with a little water in it. **Unfortunately**, the level of water was very low. **He** strained to sip the water but couldn't reach it with his beak. **Then** he tried to overturn and break the pitcher. **He** was not strong enough for that. **At** last, he spotted some small pebbles and dropped them one by one into the pitcher. **In** this way, he raised the water to the brim and quenched his thirst.

10. This fable is missing five commas. Write them in.

The Fox and the Lion

For the very first **time,** a young fox saw a lion and was ready to die of fear. The second **time,** he took courage and could even bear to look upon him. The third **time,** he came up to **him,** saluted **him,** and had a conversation with him.

11. Analyze the structure of each sentence and label its parts. Many labels will be needed more than once.

adverb

complement

object

preposition phrase

subject

verb

Labels	**subject**	**verb**	**complement**	**preposition phrase**	
a)	A crow	was	nearly dead	from thirst.	
Labels	**subject**	**verb**	**object**	**preposition phrase**	**preposition phrase**
b)	He	spied	a pitcher	with a little water	in it.
Labels	**adverb**	**subject**	**verb**	**complement**	
c)	Unfortunately,	the level of water	was	very low.	
Labels	**subject**	**verb**	**object**		
d)	He	spotted	some small pebbles.		

1.2A Dummy Subject Constructions

1. There's nothing in the world like ice cream.
   - » Ice cream is unlike anything else in the world.
2. There is no believing a liar, even when he speaks the truth.
   - » A liar cannot be believed, even when he speaks the truth.

3. To get what I want, there is nothing that I wouldn't promise.
   » To get what I want, I would promise anything.
4. There is a bone stuck in my throat.
   » A bone is stuck in my throat.
5. There are many treasures hidden in the cave.
   » Many treasures are hidden in the cave.
6. There aren't enough snacks to go around.
   » Not enough snacks are available for everyone.
7. There are no clouds in sight.
   » No clouds are in sight.
8. There are many footprints going into the lion's den, but there are none coming out.
   » Many footprints go into the lion's den, but none come out.
9. It is shocking how badly she behaves.
   » Her bad behaviour is shocking.
10. It isn't kind to say such things!
   » Such things are unkind to say.
11. It is safer to be among friends than enemies.
   » Being among friends is safer than being among enemies.
12. It's impossible to finish this on time.
   » Finishing this on time is impossible.

1.3A Parallel Structure in Lists - Fix the Errors (Level 1)

1. She enjoys hiking, jogging, and ~~to swim~~ **SWIMMING** in the lake.
2. He wants to improve his cooking skills, learn~~ing~~ to make sushi, and ~~to~~ create his own pasta dishes.
3. She wants to learn Spanish, ~~to~~ travel to Mexico, and just relax~~ing~~ on the beach.
4. To become a successful musician, you must have talent, **BE** dedicated, practice regularly, and ~~to~~ study music theory.
5. There are several solutions to pollution: clean~~ing~~ up garbage, don't drive if you don't need to, and ~~to~~ use products that are not toxic for the environment.

6. Job search websites make it is easy to search for work, upload~~ing~~ documents, and ~~communication~~ **COMMUNICATE** with potential employers.
7. Robots do things more quickly than people, like calculate large numbers, crack~~ing~~ codes, and perform~~ance of~~ actions repeatedly and accurately.
8. There are three major benefits of learning another language: enjoy**ING** foreign films, ~~communication~~ **COMMUNICATING** without barriers, and being able to work or study overseas.
9. Victims of the disease can go insane, fall into a coma, and possibly even ~~death~~ **DIE**.

1.3B Parallel Structure in Lists - Fix the Errors (Level 2)

1. In conclusion, pollution can harm our health, ~~dying~~ **KILL** creatures, and ~~it can~~ poison the soil.
2. If you want to become a nurse, you need positive qualities such as being hardworking, caring, ~~patience~~ **PATIENT** and ~~confidence~~ **CONFIDENT**.
3. As resources are consumed, forest habitats will be destroyed, species killed off, and ~~disturbing~~ indigenous people **DISTURBED**.
4. On my mom's smartphone, we can learn what the weather will be, watch~~ing~~ our favorite shows and news, or even ~~gaming~~ **GAME/PLAY GAMES**.
5. Children are constantly watching how their parents juggle work, pay the bills, and invest~~ing~~.
6. Workplace harassment can make people feel stressed, ~~poor performance~~ **PERFORM POORLY**, and want~~ing~~ to quit their job.
7. Cyberbullying can cause some teenagers to drop out socially,isolat~~ing~~ **ISOLATE** themselves, and ~~their grades drop~~ **GET LOWER GRADES**.
8. In summary, there are major differences in communication,~~our~~ lifestyle, and ~~study~~ **EDUCATION** before and after the internet.
9. The ideal job candidate must have excellent communication skills, ~~EXPERIENCED~~ **EXPERIENCE** in marketing, and ~~able~~ **THE ABILITY** to work under pressure.

1.4A Pronoun Referencing

1. **The telephone** is one of the most important inventions of all time. First, it plays a crucial role in emergency situations. For instance, ~~they allow~~ **IT ALLOWS** people to quickly contact emergency services, such as police, the fire department, or medical professionals.
2. **Humanoid robots** will soon be able to perform complex tasks on ~~its~~ **THEIR** own.
3. Once you finish sautéing the **vegetables**, put ~~it~~ **THEM** in the tortilla.
4. **Job websites** are the best solution for job seekers because ~~it lists~~ **THEY LIST** more jobs than any newspaper.
5. **Some movies** are good because ~~it is~~ **THEY ARE** funny, and we can learn a lot about life.
6. In this game, **we** collect gems and coins to unlock powers in ~~your~~ **OUR** avatar.
7. In the game, if you're not fast enough collecting **coins**, someone else will take ~~it~~ **THEM** and you have to restart the level.
8. You watch one tutorial video after another and work on the **problems** until you are able to solve ~~it~~ **THEM**.
9. **Dogs** serve different purposes to ~~its~~ **THEIR** owners.
10. **Some dogs** are aggressive and probably wouldn't be great with kids, unless ~~it is~~ **THEY ARE** well trained.

1.4B Pronoun Referencing - Fix the Errors (Level 2)

1. **Close friends** are ~~someone~~ **THOSE** you can share your hopes and dreams with. (1)
2. The problem with books is that they take up a lot of time. **People** can easily spend hours in ~~your~~ **THEIR** bedroom reading books. (1)
3. **Smartphones** have had an enormous effect on our daily lives. ~~It has~~ **THEY HAVE** given nearly all humans the ability to talk to other people anywhere in the world. (1)

4. It's not a good idea to keep exotic pets. For example, **a baby tiger** might be manageable, but when a tiger grows up, ~~they~~ **IT** can effortlessly kill ~~their~~ **ITS** owners. (2)
5. **Fake friends** don't really like you. They might be friendly at first, but later ~~she~~ **THEY** will try to take something from you. (1)
6. Laptop computers are very portable as they are compact. You can easily fit ~~it~~ **THEM** in your backpack, or you can store ~~it~~ **THEM** in your desk. (2)
7. **People** spend an unreasonable amount of time on ~~our~~ **THEIR** phones alone in ~~our~~ **THEIR** rooms. (2)
8. The sun pulls the planets to ~~it~~ **ITSELF**, so ~~it does~~ **THEY DO** not drift away. (2)
   - ITSELF is a reflexive pronoun.
     - I did it myself.
     - She did it herself.
9. Take two slices of whole wheat bread and toast ~~it~~ **THEM** for three minutes. Next, get your onion and cut ~~them~~ **IT** into small strips. (2)
10. Effluent from factories poisons the water. ~~They kill~~ **IT KILLS** a lot of marine life. (1)
11. Computers can help children with their education. Some apps, such as Word and Notes, allow ~~you~~ **THEM** to type ~~your~~ **THEIR** assignments. Others, such as Duolingo, IXL, and Grammarly, help ~~you~~ **THEM** get ahead at school. (3)

Chapter 2

2.1A Coordinating Conjunctions – Use the Correct Coordinating Conjunction to Improve This Fable

The Wolf and the Lamb

A wolf and a lamb came to a brook to quench their thirst.

The wolf stood high up the stream, **1) and/but** the lamb stood a little distance below.

The wolf made up his mind to seize the lamb, **2) so** he thought about how to justify his act of violence. He roared, "How dare you muddy the water **3) so** I cannot drink it?"

The lamb was taken aback by the accusation. She humbly responded, "the water runs down from you to me, **4) so** how could I possibly muddy it?"

The wolf retorted, "be that as it may, **5) but** you are still a rascal. You said bad things about me last year behind my back."

The lamb replied, "That's impossible! A year ago, I wasn't born, **6) so** that couldn't have been me."

"It's all the same," growled the wolf, **7) and** he jumped upon the lamb and tore her to pieces."

2.1B Coordinating Conjunctions – Use the Correct Coordinating Conjunction to Improve This Fable

The Man and His Two Sweethearts

A middle-aged man with graying hair courted two women at the same time.

One of them was young, **1) and/but** the other was well-advanced in years.

The older woman was ashamed to be courted by a younger man, **2) so** she made a point of pulling out some of his black hairs.

The younger, on the contrary, did not wish to become the wife of an old man, **3) so** she was equally zealous in removing his gray hair.

Between the two of them, he very soon lost every hair left on his head.

Try to please everybody **4) and** you will please nobody.

2.2A Correlative Conjunctions

1. **No sooner** had she started to read the book **than** she realized she had read it before.
2. **Both** the teacher **and** the students were eager to start the project.
3. **Just as** water is essential for plants, **so is** sunlight necessary for their growth.
4. I can't decide **whether** to bake a cake **or** make cookies for the dessert.
5. I would **rather** cook at home **than** risk food poisoning.
6. She was **not** upset, **but** rather surprised by the news.
7. The concert was **such** a success **that** they are planning a second show.
8. The movie was **neither** exciting **nor** interesting.
9. The museum is **not only** a place of history **but also** a center for community events.
10. The puppy is **as** playful **as** it is adorable.
11. You must **either** finish your homework **or** help with the chores.

Chapter 3

3.0A The Fisherman and the Little Fish

A fisherman **1) had been toiling** all day and **2) had caught** nothing, but as he was about to leave, he **3) pulled up** a little fish. While he **4) was reeling** it in, the fish **5) begged** him to let him go. He was small now, he said, but by and by, he would grow to be a big fish and so he would be worth catching. The fisherman **6) answered**, "No, I have you now, but I might not get you later, so it would be foolish of me to let you go."

A fish in the hand is worth two in the lake.

3.0B The Hare

Predators like dogs **1) are chasing** hares constantly. To outwit them, hares **2) possess** a good deal of cunning. Du Fouilloux, a French naturalist, **3) has reported** many interesting facts about hares.

- To escape dogs, hares **4) have joined** a flock of sheep in the field and stayed at their feet.
- Hares **5) have hidden** themselves among the rushes near a pond.
- Hares **6) have mounted** six-foot-high walls.
- When dogs **7) have been chasing** a hare for hours, the hare **8) has traded** places with another hare.

3.0C Preparing for a Career

- Exploring different hobbies and interests **1) will help** you find your true calling.
- Over the next year, you **2) will be learning/will learn** many new subjects in school.
- By the time you finish your education, you **3) will have gained** a variety of skills that employers will find valuable.

- By the time you start your first job, you **4) will have been preparing** for it for many years through your education, hobbies, and any part-time jobs.
- You **5) will meet** many people throughout your education and early career.
- During career studies at school, you **6) will be exploring/will explore** various career options. You **7) will be shaping** your understanding of different fields, so always ask questions and seek advice from teachers and professionals.
- By the time you are considering your first major career move, you **8) will have been exploring** different interests and developing skills for many years.

3.1A Identify and fix the subject-verb agreement issue in each sentence

The complete subject is underlined. The **noun/noun phrase** at the beginning determines whether the entire subject is singular/plural.

1. Compared to life in developed countries, **life** in developing countries ~~are~~ **IS** much more difficult.
2. Studies have shown that daily **screen time** for children ages 9 and up ~~have~~ **HAS** been increasing.
3. **The age group** that is most likely to get cyberbullied on social media ~~are~~ **IS** female teenagers. (DoSomething and Pew Research Center).
4. **Using** cell phones ~~are~~ **IS** disrespectful and disruptive in meetings.
5. **The transportation** of milk containers ~~are~~ **IS** done by milk tanker daily.
6. **The increasing number** of security cameras that are installed in private and government premises ~~have~~ **HAS** brought down crime rates for robberies and thefts significantly.
7. **The number** of infected patients ~~are~~ **IS** under control.
8. **The use** of devices such as cell phones, GPS watches, and trackers ~~have~~ **HAS** been gaining popularity for obvious reasons.

9. In conclusion, **the benefits** of the technologies for monitoring and tracking people clearly ~~exceeds~~ **EXCEED** the disadvantages.

3.2A Transform these sentences into their passive forms

	Passive Voice	Active Voice
1st person singular	I **am invited** to the annual gala every year.	The committee **invites** me to the annual gala every year.
2nd person singular	Every year, you **are recognized** for your athletic achievements.	Every year, the school recognizes you for your athletic achievements.
3rd person singular	She **is** often **left** at home alone while her parents travel.	Her parents often **leave** her at home alone while they travel.
1st person plural	We **are** only **informed** about policy changes at the last second.	The authorities only **inform** us about policy changes at the last second.
2nd person plural	You **are** all **appreciated** for your volunteer work.	The organization appreciates you all for your volunteer work.
3rd person plural	They **are considered** experts in their field.	Many consider them experts in their field.

3.2A Present Continuous

	Passive Voice	Active Voice
1st person singular	I'**m being given** my own department to run.	The company **is giving** me my own department to run.
2nd person singular or plural	You'**re being given** a raise next month!	The company **is giving** you a raise next month!
3rd person singular	Dinner **is being cooked** at the moment.	He'**s cooking** dinner at the moment.
1st person plural	We'**re** probably **being laid off** next month.	The company **is** probably **laying** us **off** next month.
3rd person plural	New patients **are** *now* **being accepted**.	The doctor **is** *now* **accepting** new patients.

3.3A Present Perfect

	Passive Voice	Active Voice
1st person singular	I'**ve been helped** by many people along the way.	Many people **have helped** me along the way.
2nd person singular or plural	You'**ve been given** bad information.	Somebody **has given** you bad information.
3rd person singular	Has she **been seen**?	**Has** anyone **seen** her?
1st person plural	We **haven't been told** when we'**ll be seen**.	They **haven't told** us when they will see us.
3rd person plural	They'**ve been told** to leave or the police **will be called**.	The staff **have told** them to leave or they will call the police.

3.5A Past Simple

	Passive Voice	Active Voice
1st person singular	I **was taken** to the hospital when I broke my leg.	An ambulance **took** me to the hospital when I broke my leg.
2nd person singular or plural	I'm impressed that you **were given** an award.	I'm impressed that they **gave** you an award.
3rd person singular	He **was scolded** for bad behaviour.	The teacher **scolded** him for bad behaviour.
1st person plural	We **weren't told** about the changes.	They **didn't tell** us about the changes.
3rd person plural	All the pizza slices **were eaten** by the greedy child.	The greedy child **ate** all the pizza slices!

3.5B The Mice in Council

The mice **1) (distress) were distressed** on account of their common enemy the cat, so a council **2) (call) was called** to devise means of ridding themselves of the annoyance.

Many plans **3) (propose) were proposed** and **4) (reject) rejected**. At last, **5) (suggest) it was suggested** by a young mouse that a bell be hung round the cat's neck. With advance notice of her coming, they might escape to their holes.

The proposal **6) (hail) was hailed** with applause and **7) (agree to) agreed to** unanimously. An old mouse had sat in silence, but just then got up and said, "That is well, but who will bell the cat?" The mice looked at one another, but no one answered.

The old mouse said, "It is easy to advise. What **8) (want) is wanted** is someone to act."

3.5C Cumulative Review: Passive vs Active: Present Simple, Past Simple, Present Continuous, Present Perfect

Best Studying Practices

Research has uncovered several practices that **1) (consistently use) are consistently used** by successful students.

Many students find that having their study sessions in a quiet environment **2) (lead) leads** to better focus and improved retention of information. While studying, **3) (recommend) it is recommended** that students avoid distractions such as social media or television.

In terms of whether it's better to study alone or in a group, a study **4) (conduct) was conducted** Recently which **5) (show) showed** that higher grades **6) (achieve) were achieved/are achieved** by those who study in groups at least once a week.

Currently in many schools, innovative learning methods **7) (implement) are being implemented/have been implemented** to enhance student engagement and achievement. For example, flashcards and quizzes **8) (consistently find) have consistently been found** to improve learning.

Finally, with regard to physical activity, **9) (find) it has been found** that many high achievers **10) (balance) balance** study with physical activity. This **11) (prove)**

proves that regular exercise breaks during study periods **12) (enhance) enhance** productivity and mental alertness.

3.6A Past Continuous

1. As I **was walking** home, it suddenly ***began*** to rain heavily.
2. While they **were watching** the movie, the power ***went*** out.
3. He **was reading** a book when his phone ***rang***.
4. While we **were driving** through the countryside, we ***saw*** a beautiful sunset.

3.6B Transform these sentences into their passive forms

Active Voice	Passive Voice
1. The workman broke the window while he was cleaning it.	The window ***was broken*** while it **was being cleaned**.
2. Thieves stole the sports car while its owner was storing it for the winter.	The sports car ***was stolen*** while it **was being stored** for the winter.
3. The archive staff misplaced the documents while they were archiving them.	The documents ***were misplaced*** while they **were being archived**.
4. The computer corrupted the data while the IT staff were transferring it to the new system.	The data ***was corrupted*** while it **was being transferred** to the new system.
5. Protesters vandalized the painting while a gallery was displaying it.	The painting ***was vandalized*** while it **was being displayed**.

3.7A Transform these sentences into their passive forms

Active Voice	Passive Voice
1. The committee rejected the project because the team didn't complete it on time.	The project (reject) **was rejected** because it (not complete) **had not been completed** on time.
2. She accepted the proposal because the experts had thoroughly reviewed it.	The proposal (accept) **was accepted** because it (thoroughly review) **had been thoroughly reviewed**.
3. The organizers cancelled the event because they had not raised the necessary funds.	The event (cancel) **was canceled** because the necessary funds (not raise) **had not been raised**.

4. Although the mechanic repaired the machine, the storm had severely damaged it.	Although the machine (repair) **was repaired**, it (severely damage) **had been severely damaged** during the storm.
5. They finally found the solution after they had unsuccessfully tried many alternatives.	The solution (finally find) **was finally found** after many alternatives (unsuccessfully try) **had been unsuccessfully tried**.
6. They gave the award to Dr. Mars because his lab had made groundbreaking discoveries.	The award (give) **was given** to Dr. Mars because groundbreaking discoveries (make) **had been made** in his lab.
7. They made the decision hastily after they had only discussed the problem for a few minutes.	The decision (hastily make) **was hastily made** after the problem (only discuss) **had only been discussed** for a few minutes.
8. They terminated the contract because both parties had not met the terms.	The contract (terminate) **was terminated** because the terms (not meet) **had not been met** by both parties.

3.8A Past Perfect vs Past Perfect Continuous

1. Match the sentence to its meaning:

a) I had marked the papers when you called.		3) I had completed marking the papers.
b) I was marking papers when you called.		1) You interrupted my work.
c) I had been marking papers before you called.		2) I had finished marking papers for the day.

Conjugate the verbs:

2. Yesterday when I (meet) **met** Ali, I was so tired because I (cook) **had been cooking** day.

3. When they finally (arrive) **arrived** at the hotel, they looked exhausted as they (drive) **had been driving** for over ten hours.

4. I wish I (spend) **had spent** more time studying before I (write) **wrote** that test. I'm very unhappy with my mark.

5. The garden (look) **looked** beautiful because she (take care) **had been taking care** of it all summer.

6. He (realize) **realized** he (lose) **had lost** his phone only after he got home

7. When the guests (arrive) **arrived**, the house smelled amazing because I **had been baking** (bake) all afternoon.

8. The climbers were exhausted by the time they (reach) **reached** the summit because they (climb) **had been climbing** since dawn.

9. The streets were wet when we (wake up) **woke up** because it (rain) **had been raining** all night.

10. She (feel) **felt** confident during the interview because she (prepare) **had been preparing** for weeks.

3.9A Future Simple

Active Voice	Passive Voice
1. I will write the report by Monday.	The report **will be written** by Monday.
2. They will announce the winners next week.	The winners **will be announced** next week.
3. We will plant new trees in the garden.	New trees **will be planted** in the garden.
4. The company will launch the new product in June.	The new product **will be launched** in June.
5. The chef will prepare the meal before the guests arrive.	The meal **will be prepared** before the guests arrive.
6. The students will clean the classroom after the session.	The classroom **will be cleaned** after the session.
7. The gardener will water the plants every morning.	The plants **will be watered** every morning.
8. The teacher will check the homework tomorrow.	The homework **will be checked** tomorrow.
9. The council will build a new playground in the park.	A new playground **will be built** in the park.

10. The scientists will conduct an experiment next week.	An experiment **will be conducted** next week.
11. The company will hire new employees next month.	New employees **will be hired** next month.
12. The team will solve the problem by the end of the day.	The problem **will be solved** by the end of the day.

3.11A Future Perfect

Active Voice	**Passive Voice**
1. I will have finished the assignment by tomorrow.	The assignment will have been finished by tomorrow.
2. The scientists will have synthesized a new compound by the end of this month.	A new compound will have been synthesized by the end of this month.
3. The team will have completed the project before the deadline.	The project will have been completed before the deadline.
4. The workers will have repaired the road by next week.	The road will have been repaired by next week.
5. The chef will have cooked the entire meal by 7 PM.	The entire meal will have been cooked by 7 PM.
6. We will have painted the house by the end of the month.	The house will have been painted by the end of the month.
7. The students will have submitted their essays by Friday.	The essays will have been submitted by Friday.
8. The scientists will have analyzed all the data by next Tuesday.	All the data will have been analyzed by next Tuesday.
9. The teacher will have graded all the exams by tomorrow afternoon.	All the exams will have been graded by tomorrow afternoon.
10. I will have organized the entire event by next Saturday.	The entire event will have been organized by next Saturday.

3.12A Future Perfect Continuous

1. Assuming I don't get fired, by next month, I (work) **will have been working** at this company for five years.
2. By 2030 at the latest, humanity (establish) **will have established** a permanent base on the moon.

3. By the time he retires, he (teach) **will have been teaching** for over 40 years.
4. By tomorrow morning, I (drive) **will have been driving** for ten hours straight.
5. I can't believe this crowd! By the time the movie starts, we (wait) **will have been waiting** in line for three hours.
6. I hope that by the end of this year, I (complete) **will have completed** my degree.
7. If everything goes according to plan, she (finish) **will have finished** writing her novel by the time her vacation starts.
8. She's committed to getting into this program. By the time she writes her exams next month, she (study) **will have been studying** for six months straight.
9. They (build) **will have built** the new bridge by this time next year.
10. They (reach) **will have reached** their destination by sunset.
11. We (plant) **will have planted** 100 trees by the end of this week.

Chapter 4

4.2A Subordinating Conjunctions

A wolf ran out of the forest into a village **1) because/when/since** a huntsman and a pack of hounds were after it.

The wolf saw a cat on a fence and pleaded, "My friend, which of the famers here is the kindest? I need to hide **2) while/since** my enemies are chasing me."

"Go quickly and ask Stefan," said the cat. "He is a very kind man."

"That's true, **3) although** I tore the skin off one of his sheep."

"Well, then, try Demian."

"I'm afraid he's been angry with me, too, **4) since/because/after** I carried off one of his kids."

"Run over there, then. Trofim lives there."

"Trofim! I'm afraid of even meeting him. He's been threatening to shoot me since the spring **5) when/after** I killed one of his lambs."

"Dear me, that's bad! But perhaps Klim will protect you."

"I doubt he'll protect me **6) after/since/because** I killed one of his calves earlier this year!"

"You've quarreled with the entire village," said the cat. "What sort of protection can you hope for here? These peasants would have been willing to help you **7) before** you attacked their animals, but they are not so devoid of sense as to be willing to save you now. Really, you have only yourself to blame. You're going to reap what you've sown."

4.3A The Goose with the Golden Eggs

A villager had the good fortune to possess a goose **1) that/which** laid her a golden egg each day of the year.

After a while, the woman, **2) who** had become impatient with so slow an income, killed the goose to get all at once the gold **3) that/which** she thought was inside.

When she cut her open, she was disappointed to find nothing special inside the body of the goose, **4) which** looked exactly like the body of any other goose.

Those **5) who** try to get too much can lose it all.

4.3B The Miser

1. A miser sold all that he had and bought a lump of gold, **1) which** he buried in a hole in the ground by the side of an old wall and went to look at daily.
2. One of his workmen, **2) who** observed his frequent visits to the spot, decided to watch his movements.
3. He soon discovered the secret of the hidden treasure, dug down, and found the lump of gold, **3) which** he stole.
4. The miser, **4) who** found the hole empty on his next visit, began to tear his hair and wail.
5. A neighbor, **5) who** saw him overcome with grief, asked him why he was so upset.
6. After he learned what had happened, the neighbour said, "Don't be sad. Put a stone in the hole and pretend that the gold is still lying there, **6) which** will do you the same amount of good, because when the gold was there, you didn't make the slightest use of it."

4.4A The Piglet, the Sheep, and the Goat

1. A young pig **1) that/which** was shut up in a farmyard with a goat and a sheep grunted and squeaked and resisted violently **2) when/while/as** the shepherd tried to lay hold of him.
2. The sheep and the goat, **3) which** are often handled by the farmer and do not protest, complained of his cries, **4) which** they found distressing.

3. To this the pig replied, "Our situations are very different **5) because/ since/as** he catches you only for your wool or your milk **6) while/ although** he lays hold of me for my very life."

4.5.3A Parallel Structure in Comparisons - Fix the Errors (Level 2)

1. Mia's slice of cake is large while Jenny**'S** is small.
2. In many rich countries, the food quality is worse than **IN** poor countries.
3. In many rich countries, the food quality is worse than poor countrie**s'**.
4. I believe work experience is equal to or sometimes more valuable than ~~educated people~~

EDUCATION.

1. Italy's land area is about 294,000 square kilometers while Spain**'S** is about 499,000 square kilometers.

4.5.3B Parallel Structure in Comparisons - Fix the Errors (Level 3)

1. When you get older, you will need to face more challenging work than **IN** your previous school years.

2. High schools in China apply class rankings to compare students' grades with their classmate**s'**.

3. According to research by universities, cheating incidents in 2019 were 50% more common than **IN** the year before.

4. Many social media users only post the best parts of their life, which may make children think that their lives are not as good as other**s'**.

5. The only problem with my new place is that the kitchen is smaller than **IN** my previous place.

6. People in big cities have more flexibility in their careers compared to **THOSE IN** small cities.

7. People with good communication skills are 70% more likely to get promoted than those ~~who do not~~ **WITHOUT THEM**.

Chapter 5

5.2A Conjugate these verbs using present unreal conditional

1. If I (win) **won** the lottery, I (buy) **would buy** a sports car.
2. If I (be) **were** you, I (not eat) **wouldn't eat** that stinky shrimp.
3. If it (not be) **weren't** so cold, we (can go) **could go** outside.
4. If I (not be) **weren't** so tired, I (be) **would be** more productive.
5. I (probably meet) **would probably** more people if I (not spend) **didn't spend** all my time playing video games.
6. If the government (introduce) **introduced** a tax on all plastic bags in supermarkets, this (start) **would start** to add up and people (notice) **would notice** it by the time they (get) **got** to the cash register. Then, people (think) **would think** about the amount of plastic they use when buying food and this (lead) **would lead** to less garbage being produced.
7. I (get) **would get** higher marks if I (study) **studied** more.
8. If the weather (be) **were** nice, we (go) **could go** for a walk.
9. She's not doing too well. If she (have) **had** proper medical treatment, she (recover) **would recover** quickly.
10. If it (be) **were** summer, we (can spend) **could spend** more time outside.
11. I (meet) **would meet** more people if I (go out) **went** instead of spending all my time online.

5.3A Conjugate these verbs using past unreal conditional

1. If you (show up) **had shown up** on time, we (not be) **wouldn't have been** late.
2. The meeting was cancelled. If I (know) **had known** earlier, I (sleep in) **would have slept in**.
3. No, I didn't end up buying a real Burberry. If it (be) **had been** cheaper, I (get) **would have gotten** it. I ended up getting a knockoff instead for a fraction of the price.

That's a really nice one! If you (not tell) **hadn't told** me it's a fake, I (never guess) **never would have guessed**.

1. My project partners were so lazy. I (be) **would've been** better off doing the project alone.
2. The hack (not happen) **wouldn't have happened** if he (have) **had had** a stronger password than "ABC123."
3. She is now a successful art teacher and she (might not develop) **might not have developed** this skill if she (not have) **hadn't had** such great teachers.
4. If my father (not push) **hadn't pushed** me to get a job, I (might not learn) **might not have learned** the value of hard work at such a young age.
5. If he (never change) **had never changed** his career, his business (stop be) **would have stopped being** successful and he (not discover) **wouldn't have discovered** a passion for what he's doing now.
6. If I (not oversleep) **hadn't overslept** this morning, I (not miss) **wouldn't have missed** my bus.

5.4A Conjugate these verbs using past and present unreal conditional

1. If I **(know) had known** what I know now, I **(not be) wouldn't be** in this mess.
2. If it **(not be) weren't** for this traffic jam, we **(arrive) would have arrived** at the conference an hour ago.
3. If I **(buy) had bought** those Google shares when Google was brand new, I definitely **(not work) wouldn't be working** at this crappy job.
4. If I **(not eat) hadn't eaten** that stinky shrimp for lunch earlier today, I **(not have) wouldn't have** a horrible stomachache right now.
5. If I **(not quit) hadn't quit** my job, I **(not have) wouldn't have** my own business now.
6. I **(be) would be** better prepared for this test tomorrow if I **(study) had studied** more over the past few weeks.
7. If I **(not party) hadn't partied** in Las Vegas last weekend, I **(not be) wouldn't be** broke now.

Chapter 6

6.1A Use an appropriate conjunctive adverb to complete each sentence.

1. The hare boasted about his speed; **however,** the tortoise's steady pace won the race in the end.
2. The lion spared the mouse's life; **consequently,** the mouse later freed the lion from a hunter's net.
3. The ant worked hard all summer storing food; **meanwhile,** the grasshopper sang and danced without a care.
4. The fox praised the crow's singing; **thus**, when replying, the crow dropped the cheese, and the fox quickly snatched it up.
5. The dog barked at his reflection in the water; **hence/consequently/as a result/thus,** he lost the bone he was carrying in his mouth.
6. The thirsty crow found a tall pitcher with a little water; **therefore,** he dropped pebbles into it until the water rose high enough to drink.
7. The peacock flaunted his beautiful feathers; **meanwhile,** the crane flew gracefully above, unimpressed by the display.
8. The wolf disguised himself in sheep's clothing to blend in with the flock; **eventually,** the shepherd discovered the ruse and chased him away.
9. The boy cried "wolf" too many times as a joke; **hence,** when a real wolf appeared, no one came to his aid.
10. The farmer discovered that the goose laid golden eggs; **consequently,** in his greed, he killed the goose, finding no more gold inside.

Chapter 7

7.1A Transform these simple sentence pairs into complex sentences using Type I Relative Clauses

1. The cat is sitting on the windowsill. It is watching the birds outside.
   - The cat, which is sitting on the windowsill, is watching the birds outside.
   - The cat, which is watching the birds outside, is sitting on the windowsill.
2. Marisse read a book last night. It was extremely interesting.
   - Marisse read a book that was extremely interesting last night.
   - Marisse read a book which was extremely interesting last night.
   - The book that Marisse read last night was extremely interesting.
   - The book which Marisse read last night was extremely interesting.
   - The book Marisse read last night was extremely interesting.
3. My friend moved to New York last year. He is visiting us next weekend.
   - My friend, who moved to New York last year, is visiting us next weekend.
   - My friend, who is visiting us next weekend, moved to New York last year.
4. The old tree has been there for over a hundred years. It's in the middle of the park.
   - The old tree, which is in the middle of the park, has been there for over a hundred years.
   - The old tree which is in the middle of the park has been there for over a hundred years.
   - The old tree that's in the middle of the park has been there for over a hundred years.

5. She chose a dress for her performance. It sparkled under the lights.
    - She chose a dress that sparkled under the lights for her performance.
    - She chose a dress which sparkled under the lights for her performance.
6. Gennady teaches mathematics. He is known for his engaging lessons.
    - Gennady, who teaches mathematics, is known for his engaging lessons.
    - Gennady, who is known for his engaging lessons, teaches mathematics.
7. This is the restaurant. It received the best reviews in town.
    - This is the restaurant which received the best reviews in town.
    - This is the restaurant that received the best reviews in town.
8. He found a wallet. It belonged to someone in the next building.
    - He found a wallet that belonged to someone in the next building.
    - He found a wallet which belonged to someone in the next building.
9. We watched a movie last night. It was based on a true story.
    - The movie which we watched last night was based on a true story.
    - The movie that we watched last night was based on a true story.
    - The movie we watched last night was based on a true story.
10. Dr. Mars won the award. He is known for his groundbreaking research.
    - Dr. Mars, who won the award, is known for his groundbreaking research.
    - Dr. Mars, who is known for his groundbreaking research, won the award.

7.2A Transform these simple sentence pairs into complex sentences using Type II Relative Clauses

1. The girl is calling for her cat to come down. Her cat climbed the tallest tree in the neighborhood.
    » The girl whose cat climbed the tallest tree in the neighborhood is calling for it to come down.

2. I met a museum curator. His passion for ancient history inspired several generations of children.
   » I met a museum curator whose passion for ancient history inspired several generations of children.
3. She borrowed a book from the library. Its pages were almost a hundred years old.
   » She borrowed a book whose pages were almost a hundred years old from the library.
4. The teacher received an award for excellence in teaching. His lessons are always engaging.
   » The teacher, whose lessons are always engaging, received an award for excellence in teaching.
5. The artist Yasho's work is displayed in the city gallery. He is known for his abstract paintings.
   » The artist Yasho, whose work is displayed in the city gallery, is known for his abstract paintings.
6. We visited a museum. Its collection of artifacts spans over two thousand years.
   » We visited a museum whose collection of artifacts spans over two thousand years.
7. She wore a dress. Its fabric shimmered under the ballroom lights.
   » She wore a dress whose fabric shimmered under the ballroom lights.
8. This bakery attracts customers from all over town. Its bread is known for its authentic French taste.
   » This bakery, whose bread is known for its authentic French taste, attracts customers from all over town.

7.3A Transform these simple sentence pairs into complex sentences using Type III Relative Clauses

1. Thank you for your help. Without it, I couldn't have finished this project.

    - Thank you for your help, **without which** I couldn't have finished this project.
    - Thank you for your help, **which** I couldn't have finished this project **without**.

2. I don't remember the man. I got the message from him.

    - I don't remember the man **from whom** I got the message.
    - I don't remember the man **whom** I got the message **from**.
    - I don't remember the man I got the message from.

3. I can't remember the supplier. We got that part from them last year.

    - I can't remember the supplier **from which** we got that part last year.
    - I can't remember the supplier **which** we got that part **from** last year.
    - I can't remember the supplier we got that part from last year.

4. That's the village. I grew up in that village.

    - That's the village **in which** I grew up.
    - That's the village **which** I grew up **in**.
    - That's the village **where** I grew up.
        - » where = in which/on which

5. That's the farm. I grew up on that farm.

    - That's the farm **on which** I grew up.
    - That's the farm **which** I grew up **on**.
    - That's the farm **where** I grew up.
        - » where = in which/on which

6. He showed me the powerful computer. He designs his complex architectural models on it.

    - He showed me the powerful computer **on which** he designs his complex architectural models.

- He showed me the powerful computer **which** he designs his complex architectural models **on.**

7. They moved to a new city. They knew very little about it.

- They moved to a new city **about which** they knew very little.
- They moved to a new city **which** they knew very little **about**.

8. She passed on the message to her colleague Steve. She collaborates on important projects with him.

- She passed on the message to her colleague Steve, **with whom** she collaborates on important projects.
- She passed on the message to her colleague Steve, **whom** she collaborates on important projects **with**.

9. He found a wallet. There was a rare old coin inside it.

- He found a wallet **inside which** there was a rare old coin.
- He found a wallet **which** there was a rare old coin **inside**.

10. That's the old alleyway. We used to play there as children.

- That's the old alleyway **in which** we used to play as children.
- That's the old alleyway **which** we used to play **in** as children.
- That's the old alleyway **where** we used to play as children.
  - » where = in which

7.3B Transform these simple sentence pairs into complex sentences using Type III Relative Clauses

1. The CEO announced major changes. In response to these changes, many employees have voiced their concerns.
   - » The CEO announced major changes, **in response to which** many employees have voiced their concerns.
2. The match was postponed. On account of this postponement, fans were offered refunds or tickets to the rescheduled game.
   - » The match was postponed, **on account of which** fans were offered refunds or tickets to the rescheduled game.

3. The community center was named after a local hero. In honor of him, a special ceremony was organized.
   » The community center was named after a local hero, **in honor of whom** a special ceremony was organized.
4. The river flows through the town. By the side of the river, children love to play during the summer.
   » The river flows through the town, **by the side of which** children love to play during the summer.
5. Crazy new evidence was presented at trial yesterday. In light of this evidence, the case took a completely different turn.
   » Crazy new evidence was presented at trial yesterday, in light of which the case took a completely different turn.
6. The city council passed a new environmental policy. As a result of this policy, local businesses started adopting green practices.
   » The city council passed a new environmental policy**, as a result of which** local businesses started adopting green practices.
7. The company introduced new software. With the help of this software, productivity increased significantly.
   » The company introduced new software**, with the help of which** productivity increased significantly.
8. The library was established centuries ago. Within the confines of the library, countless rare manuscripts are preserved.
   » The library was established centuries ago**, within the confines of which** countless rare manuscripts are preserved.
9. The researchers gained access to unique data. By virtue of this data, they were able to draw groundbreaking conclusions.
   » The researchers gained access to unique data**, by virtue of which** they were able to draw groundbreaking conclusions.

10. The team had to work without their lead analyst. In the absence of the lead analyst, they faced significant challenges in completing the project.
    » The team had to work without their lead analyst, **in the absence of whom** they faced significant challenges in completing the project.

7.4A Transform these simple sentence pairs into complex sentences using Type IV Relative Clauses

1. The bakery sold 100 specialty cupcakes in an hour. **A quarter of them** were chocolate flavored.
    » The bakery sold 100 specialty cupcakes in an hour, **a quarter of which** were chocolate flavored.
    » The bakery sold 100 specialty cupcakes in an hour, **of which a quarter** were chocolate flavored.
2. The library acquired 300 new books last month. **Half of them** are on science and technology.
    » The library acquired 300 new books last month, half of which are on science and technology.
    » The library acquired 300 new books last month, **of which half** are on science and technology.
3. Our class has 25 students. **Four of them** have birthdays in July.
    » Our class has 25 students, four of whom have birthdays in July.
    » Our class has 25 students, **of whom four** have birthdays in July.
4. The zoo trip was exciting for the 30 children. **Most of them** saw a lion for the first time.
    » The zoo trip was exciting for the 30 children, **most of whom** saw a lion for the first time.

5. The survey received responses from 200 participants. **Nearly 60% of them** expressed satisfaction with the service.
   » The survey received responses from 200 participants, nearly 60% of whom expressed satisfaction with the service.
   » The survey received responses from 200 participants, **of whom nearly 60%** expressed satisfaction with the service.
6. They planned an expensive school field trip. **The cost of the trip** was covered by a bake sale fundraiser.
   » They planned an expensive school field trip, **the cost of which** was covered by a bake sale fundraiser.
7. The unexpected freeze lasted for weeks. **The effects** were damaged crops.
   » The unexpected freeze lasted for weeks, **the effects of which** were damaged crops.
8. They discovered an ancient artifact. **The surface** was inscribed with unknown symbols.
   » They discovered an ancient artifact, **the surface of which** was inscribed with unknown symbols.
9. The company implemented a new policy. **The consequence** was a significant increase in employee productivity.
   » The company implemented a new policy, **the consequence of which** was a significant increase in employee productivity.
10. The magician performed a trick. He promised to reveal **the secret** at the end of the show.
   » The magician performed a trick, **the secret of which** he promised to reveal at the end of the show.

7.5A Transform these simple sentence pairs into complex sentences using Type V Relative Clauses

1. We'd like to show our appreciation for the parent council. Without their help, we couldn't have bought this new sports equipment.
   » We'd like to show our appreciation for the parent council, **without whose help** we couldn't have bought this new sports equipment.
2. I'd like to congratulate the team. Without their commitment to practice, this victory would never have happened.
   » I'd like to congratulate the team, **without whose commitment** to practice this victory would never have happened.
3. The team was led by Dr. Mars. Under his guidance, they achieved remarkable success.
   » The team was led by Dr. Mars**, under whose guidance** they achieved remarkable success.
4. We need to fire the company president. As a result of her errors, we now face bankruptcy.
   » We need to fire the company president, **as a result of whose** errors we now face bankruptcy.
5. We owe a lot to the librarian. Without her creativity, we wouldn't have had such engaging events.
   » We owe a lot to the librarian, **without whose creativity** we wouldn't have had such engaging events.

7.6A Each example below contains a misplaced modifier. Identify it and move it to a better spot in the sentence

Level 1

1. Some animals are specially adapted to cold weather, like polar bears and arctic wolves.
   » Some animals **like polar bears and arctic wolves** are specially adapted to cold weather.
2. Many sports involve physical contact such as hockey and football.
   » Many sports **such as hockey and football** involve physical contact.

3. Endangered animals are killed for money, such as rhinos and elephants.
   » Endangered animals **such as rhinos and elephants** are killed for money.
4. The goal was set by the legendary king, of bringing peace to the entire kingdom.
   » The goal **of bringing peace to the entire kingdom** was set by the legendary king.

Level 2

1. She used to play computer games after she finished her homework for hours.
   » She used to play computer games **for hours** after she finished her homework.
2. Different pharaohs had visions for developing Egypt, such as Akhenaton, Queen Hatshepsut, and Ramses II.
   » Different pharaohs**, such as Akhenaton, Queen Hatshepsut, and Ramses II,** had visions for developing Egypt.
3. Great art cannot be imitated easily, like Rembrandt's or Titian's.
   » Great art**, like Rembrandt's or Titian's,** cannot be imitated easily.
4. Sitting in front of the screen the whole day has become a trend among teenagers in the last few years to play and talk with peers instead of going outdoors.
   » Sitting in front of the screen the whole day **to play and talk with peers instead of going outdoors** has become a trend among teenagers **in the last few years**.

Level 3

1. In the US, most people are not fit, which has an obesity rate of 36.2%.
   » In the US**, which has an obesity rate of 36.2%,** most people are not fit.

2. Only a few species like sandfish can survive in dunes, which are a type of lizard that can swim through the smooth sand.
   » Only a few species like sandfish**, which are a type of lizard that can swim through the smooth sand,** can survive in dunes.
3. Another ride at the amusement park was also fast, but this time it made you rise into the air which I think was called The Umbrella.
   » Another ride at the amusement park**, which I think was called The Umbrella,** was also fast, but this time it made you rise into the air.
4. Plastic waste is definitely the main factor behind the devastation of our oceans and land, which is discarded by thoughtless people.
   » Plastic waste**, which is discarded by thoughtless people,** is definitely the main factor behind the devastation of our oceans and land.
5. Government revenue in Japan increased when the Olympic games were held there by 120 trillion yen.
   » Government revenue in Japan increased **by 120 trillion yen** when the Olympic games were held there.

Chapter 9

9.1A Transform these simple and complex sentences into sentences with participial phrases

Answers

1. The scientist made a discovery. It changed our understanding of the world.
   » The scientist made a discovery, changing our understanding of the world.
2. Since she practiced piano every day, she became an exceptional player.
   » Practicing piano every day, she became an exceptional player.
3. He wrote a well-researched essay that impressed all his teachers.
   » He wrote a well-researched essay, impressing all his teachers.
4. After they finally completed the project, they felt a sense of accomplishment.
   » Finally completing the project, they felt a sense of accomplishment.
   » After finally completing the project, they felt a sense of accomplishment.
5. Lightning struck the old oak tree. It caused a large branch to fall.
   » Lightning struck the old oak tree, causing a large branch to fall.
6. The artist who's painting the mural is famous in the community.
   » The artist painting the mural is famous in the community.
7. The dog barked loudly. It alerted the neighbors.
   » The dog barked loudly, alerting the neighbors.
8. While she was reading the novel, she discovered a hidden message.
   » Reading the novel, she discovered a hidden message.
   » While reading the novel, she discovered a hidden message.

9. The students who completed the extra credit assignments raised their grades significantly.
   » The students completing the extra credit assignments raised their grades significantly.
   » Completing the extra credit assignments, the students raised their grades significantly.
10. The volcano erupted last night. It spewed lava and ash over the village.
   » The volcano erupted last night, spewing lava and ash over the village.
11. The musician who played the violin captivated the audience.
   » The musician playing the violin captivated the audience.
   » Playing the violin, the musician captivated the audience.
12. Despite the fact that group projects can foster teamwork, they're often unproductive.
   » Despite fostering teamwork, group projects are often unproductive.

9.2A Combine these simple sentences into complex sentences with passive participial phrases

1. He received the scholarship. It had been established by a local entrepreneur.
   » He received the scholarship established by a local entrepreneur.
2. She discovered her necklace. It had been lost during the school trip.
   » She discovered her necklace, lost during the school trip.
3. The museum unveiled the painting. It had been restored carefully over the last year.
   » The museum unveiled the painting, carefully restored over the last year.
4. The shelter took in several animals. They had been rescued from abandoned homes.
   » The shelter took in several animals rescued from abandoned homes.

5. The artifact was returned to the museum. It had been stolen by thieves.
    » The artifact, stolen by thieves, was returned to the museum.
6. The concert was cancelled. It had been scheduled for Friday night.
    » The concert, scheduled for Friday night, was cancelled.
7. The proposal was finally accepted. It had been submitted three months ago.
    » The proposal, submitted three months ago, was finally accepted.
8. The team won the championship. They had been considered underdogs all season.
    » The team, considered underdogs all season, won the championship.
9. The building was evacuated safely. It had been threatened by the approaching storm.
    » The building, threatened by the approaching storm, was evacuated safely.
10. The documentary was aired on national television. It had been produced by local students.
    » The documentary, produced by local students, was aired on national television.
11. The athlete was awarded the gold medal. He had been disqualified in the previous competition.
    » The athlete, disqualified in the previous competition, was awarded the gold medal.
12. The painting was sold at auction for millions of dollars. It had been considered hideous by art critics.
    » The painting, considered hideous by art critics, was sold at auction for millions of dollars.

9.3A Combine these simple sentences into complex sentences with passive participial phrases that begin with after, before, while, and despite

1. Before the video game was released by the developers, it was beta-tested by gamers around the world.
   » Before being released by the developers, the video game was beta-tested by gamers around the world.
2. After the novel was read by the book club, it was discussed in a lively meeting.
   » After being read by the book club, the novel was discussed in a lively meeting.
3. Before he was sent on the trip, he was given secret instructions.
   » Before being sent on the trip, he was given secret instructions.
4. After the essay was reviewed by the teacher, it was returned with suggestions for improvement.
   » After being reviewed by the teacher, the essay was returned with suggestions for improvement.
5. After the recipe was perfected by the chef, it was added to the restaurant's menu.
   » After being perfected by the chef, the recipe was added to the restaurant's menu.
6. While he was being arrested, the suspect bit the police officer.
   » While being arrested, the suspect bit the police officer.
7. Before he was elected prime minister, Justin Trudeau was a drama teacher.
   » Before being elected prime minister, Justin Trudeau was a drama teacher.

8. Despite the fact that plastic bags are commonly used today, they're not ideal for environmental sustainability.
   » Despite plastic bags being commonly used today, they're not ideal for environmental sustainability.
   » Despite being commonly used today, plastic bags are not ideal for environmental sustainability.

9.3C Combine these simple sentences into complex sentences with perfect participial phrases starting with ***with***

1. The city allocated $5 million to public park improvements last year. $2 million of this budget was used for playground upgrades and the rest for landscaping.
   » The city allocated $5 million to public park improvements last year, **with** $2 million **going** to playground upgrades and the rest to landscaping.
2. In the survey, 90% of participants expressed concern about climate change. However, only 50% reported changing their daily habits to reduce their carbon footprint.
   » In the survey, 90% of participants expressed concern about climate change, **with** only 50% **reporting** changes in their daily habits to reduce their carbon footprint.
3. I'm comfortable if the team starts the project without me.
   » I'm comfortable **with** the team **starting** the project without me.
4. The school announced a new online learning platform this semester. 70% of the feedback from students and parents has been positive.
   » The school announced a new online learning platform this semester, **with** 70% of the feedback from students and parents **being** positive.
5. Nearly 60% of the workforce has transitioned to remote work. Only 10% report a preference for the office environment.
   » Nearly 60% of the workforce has transitioned to remote work, **with** only 10% **reporting** a preference for the office environment.

6. The committee approved the budget for the next fiscal year. However, some members expressed concerns about the allocation for health services.
   » The committee approved the budget for the next fiscal year, **with** some members, however, **expressing** concerns about the allocation for health services.
7. The new software update was released last night. Many users are reporting issues with installation.
   » The new software update was released last night, **with** many users **reporting** issues with installation.
8. I'm disappointed because the project is delayed again.
   » I'm disappointed **with** the project **being** delayed again.
9. The company achieved a 15% increase in sales this quarter. This success is largely attributed to the new marketing campaign.
   » The company achieved a 15% increase in sales this quarter, **with** the success **being** largely attributed to the new marketing campaign.

9.4A Combine these simple sentences into complex sentences with perfect participial phrases

1. Because I've read the entire book series, I can discuss all the plot twists and character developments.
   » Having read the entire book series, I can discuss all the plot twists and character developments.
2. Because I haven't finished my homework, I can't go out with my friends tonight.
   » Not having finished my homework, I can't go out with my friends tonight.
3. I have listened to this musician many times. I'm familiar with his work.
   » Having listened to this musician many times, I'm familiar with his work.

4. Serena Williams has won multiple Grand Slam titles. She is considered one of the greatest tennis players of all time.
   » Having won multiple Grand Slam titles, Serena Williams is considered one of the greatest tennis players of all time.
   » Serena Williams, having won multiple Grand Slam titles, is considered one of the greatest tennis players of all time.
5. I have researched the topic extensively. I am prepared to lead the discussion in tomorrow's meeting.
   » Having researched the topic extensively, I am prepared to lead the discussion in tomorrow's meeting.
6. I haven't visited the new museum exhibit yet. I can't give you a personal opinion about it.
   » Not having visited the new museum exhibit yet, I can't give you a personal opinion about it.
7. The team had lost three games in a row. They practiced even harder to break the losing streak.
   » Having lost three games in a row, the team practiced even harder to break the losing streak.
8. She had studied abroad in Japan for a year. She brought back unique perspectives to her studies.
   » Having studied abroad in Japan for a year, she brought back unique perspectives to her studies.
9. They had completed the marathon despite the bad weather. They felt a tremendous sense of achievement.
   » Having completed the marathon despite the bad weather, they felt a tremendous sense of achievement.
10. I had researched the topic for months. I was ready to present my findings at the conference.
    » Having researched the topic for months, I was ready to present my findings at the conference.

11. He had never traveled outside of his home country. He was thrilled about his upcoming trip.
    - Having never traveled outside of his home country, he was thrilled about his upcoming trip.
    - Never having traveled outside of his home country, he was thrilled about his upcoming trip.
12. We had watched all the tutorials available. We started creating our own videos.
    - Having watched all the tutorials available, we started creating our own videos.

9.5A Combine these simple sentences into complex sentences with perfect passive participial phrases

1. The new policies have been approved by the government. They will be implemented starting next month.
    - **Having been approved** by the government, the new policies will be implemented starting next month.
2. The software has been updated by the development team. It now includes new security features.
    - **Having been updated** by the development team, the software now includes new security features.
3. The lost kitten has been found by the neighborhood kids. It's safe at home now.
    - **Having been found** by the neighborhood kids, the lost kitten is safe at home now.
4. The science fair projects have been evaluated by the teachers. The best projects will go to the regional competition.
    - **Having been evaluated** by the teachers, the best science fair projects will go to the regional competition.

5. The player has been accused of doping, so he is waiting at home pending drug test results.
   » **Having been accused** of doping, the player is waiting at home pending drug test results.
6. We have been given the day off, so we are going for a long bike ride.
   » **Having been given** the day off, we are going for a long bike ride.
7. She was made redundant. She had to start looking for a new job.
   » **Having been made** redundant, she had to start looking for a new job.
8. The novel has been translated into thirty languages. It is now accessible worldwide.
   » **Having been translated** into thirty languages, the novel is now accessible worldwide.
9. The old mansion has been renovated by the city. It serves as a museum now.
   » **Having been renovated** by the city, the old mansion now serves as a museum.
10. The documentary has been viewed by millions. It sparked a global conversation on this controversial topic.
   » **Having been viewed** by millions, the documentary sparked a global conversation on this controversial topic.

Chapter 10

10.1A Rewrite these sentences so that each one contains a noun clause. The new sentences should have the same meaning as the originals

1. Who will lead the project next month? Can you explain this to me?
   - » Can you explain who will lead the project next month?
2. She couldn't remember her breakfast this morning.
   - » She couldn't remember what she had for breakfast this morning.
3. They are discussing their vacation plans. They aren't sure of a location to go to.
   - » They are discussing where to go for a vacation.
4. He asked about my job start date.
   - » He asked me when I start the new job.
5. She questioned the decision. Why was it made without her?
   - » She questioned why the decision was made without her.
6. How did they solve the problem? Can you show me?
   - » Can you show me how they solved the problem?
7. The competition winner will receive a scholarship.
   - » Whoever wins the competition will receive a scholarship.
8. What did he tell you? Tell me everything.
   - » Tell me whatever he told you.
9. Her fluency in three languages is surprising.
   - » It's surprising that she is fluent in three languages.
10. Do you know the owner of the notebook that was left on the table?
    - » Do you know whose notebook was left on the table?

Chapter 11

11.1A Rewrite these sentences so that each one contains subjunctive mood. The new sentences should have the same meaning as the originals

1. You should inform him of the decision immediately.
   - I ask that he be informed of the decision immediately.
2. The lawyer demanded, "release my client from custody."
   - The lawyer demanded that her client be released from custody.
3. She says, "everyone needs to arrive on time for the meeting."
   - She insists that everyone arrive on time for the meeting.
4. The judge ordered the evidence to be presented by tomorrow.
   - The judge ordered that the evidence be presented by tomorrow.
5. The doctor says, "take the medication twice a day."
   - The doctor recommends that you take the medication twice a day.
6. He said, "she should study more if she wants to pass the exam."
   - He suggests that she study more if she wants to pass the exam.
7. The company requires all employees to undergo annual training.
   - The company requires that all employees undergo annual training.
8. Please deliver this package by noon.
   - I request that this package be delivered by noon.
9. They advise travelers to check weather conditions before departing.
   - They advise that travelers check weather conditions before departing.
10. He said, "take a different route to avoid traffic."
    - He proposed that we take a different route to avoid traffic.
11. It is essential for everyone to remain calm during the drill.
    - It is essential that everyone remain calm during the drill.
12. You are advised to save your work frequently to avoid data loss.
    - It is advised that you save your work frequently to avoid data loss.

13. Following the instructions to the letter is crucial to ensure safety.
    - » It is crucial that the instructions be followed to the letter to ensure safety.
14. I would like you to keep this information confidential until the announcement.
    - » I would ask that you keep this information confidential until the announcement.
15. Acting now to prevent further damage is vital.
    - » It is vital that we act now to prevent further damage.

Chapter 12

12.1A Rewrite these sentences so that each one contains an appositive. The new sentences should have the same meaning as the originals

1. My brother, who is an engineer, works in a multinational company.
   » My brother, an engineer, works in a multinational company.
2. Leonardo da Vinci, who was a renowned painter, also excelled in engineering.
   » Leonardo da Vinci, a renowned painter, also excelled in engineering.
3. Mount Everest, which is the highest mountain in the world, attracts numerous climbers every year.
   » Mount Everest, the highest mountain in the world, attracts numerous climbers every year.
4. The novel "War and Peace", which is a masterpiece written by Leo Tolstoy, is considered one of the greatest books of all time.
   » The novel "War and Peace," a masterpiece by Leo Tolstoy, is considered one of the greatest books of all time.
5. Albert Einstein, who developed the theory of relativity, is one of the most famous scientists in history.
   » Albert Einstein, the developer of the theory of relativity, is one of the most famous scientists in history.
6. "The Scream," which was painted by Edvard Munch, has become an iconic symbol of existential angst.
   » "The Scream," a painting by Edvard Munch, has become an iconic symbol of existential angst.
7. Wolfgang Amadeus Mozart, who was a prolific and influential composer, left a significant mark on the history of Western music.
   » Wolfgang Amadeus Mozart, a prolific and influential composer, significantly impacted Western music history.

8. The Tesla Roadster, which is an electric sports car, can accelerate from 0 to 60 mph in just 1.9 seconds.
    » The Tesla Roadster, an electric sports car, can accelerate from 0 to 60 mph in just 1.9 seconds.
9. The Sphinx, which is a mythical creature with the body of a lion and the head of a human, is a symbol of ancient Egypt.
    » The Sphinx, a mythical creature with the body of a lion and the head of a human, symbolizes ancient Egypt.
10. The Great Barrier Reef, which is the world's largest coral reef system, is home to thousands of marine species.
    » The Great Barrier Reef, the world's largest coral reef system, is home to thousands of marine species.

12.2. Rewrite these sentences so that each one contains an adjective cluster or phrase. The new sentences should have the same meaning as the originals

1. The cat moved silently across the garden. It was sleek and shadowy. It was alert for any sign of movement.
    » The cat, sleek and shadowy, moved silently across the garden, alert for any sign of movement.
2. He handed in his resignation. He was firm in his decision. He was ready for a new beginning.
    » He handed in his resignation, firm in his decision and ready for a new beginning.
    » He handed in his resignation, firm in his decision, ready for a new beginning.
3. The garden was blooming. It was full of vibrant colors and the sweet scent of spring flowers.
    » The garden was blooming, full of vibrant colors and the sweet scent of spring flowers.

4. The old museum finally opened its doors after a long renovation. It's rich in history and alive with the stories of the past.
   - » The old museum, rich in history and alive with the stories of the past, finally opened its doors after a long renovation.
5. The old library book held secrets of the past. It was worn and fragile.
   - » The old library book, worn and fragile, held secrets of the past.
6. Her new song played on the radio everywhere for months. It was catchy and uplifting.
   - » Her new song, catchy and uplifting, played on the radio everywhere for months.
7. The puppy raced across the yard. It was small, fluffy, and energetic. It was eager to play with anyone who would give it attention.
   - » The puppy, small, fluffy, and energetic, raced across the yard, eager to play with anyone who would give it attention.
8. She finished her painting. She was proud of her work. However, she was anxious about displaying it at the school art show.
   - » She finished her painting, proud of her work but anxious about displaying it at the school art show.
9. The children were ready to dive into the latest story. They were full of anticipation.
   - » The children, full of anticipation, were ready to dive into the latest story.
10. The undefeated basketball team entered the gym. They were confident in their ability to win the championship.
    - » The undefeated basketball team entered the gym, confident in their ability to win the championship.

Chapter 13

13.1A Combine these sentences by transforming one of them into a nominative absolute.

1. The city arose from the desert. The gleaming towers **were** a sign of economic progress.
   - » The city arose from the desert, the gleaming towers a sign of economic progress.
2. She glared at him in silence. The only sound **was** the ticking clock.
   - » She glared at him in silence, the only sound the ticking clock.
   - » She glared at him in silence, with the only sound the ticking clock.
3. She listened intently to the music. The notes **were** as sweet as honey.
   - » She listened intently to the music, the notes as sweet as honey.
4. They admired the painting. Its colours **were** as vibrant as a rainbow.
   - » They admired the painting, its colours as vibrant as a rainbow.
5. He watched the waves crash against the shore. The sound **was** as soothing as a lullaby.
   - » He watched the waves crash against the shore, the sound as soothing as a lullaby.
6. He went for a walk. A hat **was** on his head to protect him against the sun.
   - » He went for a walk, a hat on his head to protect him against the sun.
7. The security guard stood there impassively. His uniform **was** crisp and clean.
   - » The security guard stood there impassively, his uniform crisp and clean.
8. The concert **was** over. The crowd filed out of the arena.
   - » The concert over, the crowd filed out of the arena.
   - » With the concert over, the crowd filed out of the arena.
9. The game **was** won. The team celebrated with high-fives and cheers.
   - » The game won, the team celebrated with high-fives and cheers.
   - » With the game won, the team celebrated with high-fives and cheers.

13.2A Combine these sentences by transforming one of them into a nominative absolute

1. We hiked through the forest. The leaves rustled beneath our feet.
    » We hiked through the forest, **the leaves rustling** beneath our feet.
2. They floated down the river. The water gently carried them along.
    » They floated down the river, **the water gently carrying** them along.
3. He marched down the street. His boots clunked on the pavement.
    » He marched down the street, **his boots clunking** on the pavement.
4. She skated across the rink. Her blades glided smoothly over the ice.
    » She skated across the rink, **her blades gliding** smoothly over the ice.
5. She drove away in the sports car. The engine roared as she shifted gears.
    » She drove away in the sports car, **the engine roaring** as she shifted gears.
6. The chef prepared a delectable dish. Its aroma filled the entire restaurant.
    » The chef prepared a delectable dish, **its aroma filling** the entire restaurant.
7. We trekked up the mountain. The rocks shifted and slid beneath our boots.
    » We trekked up the mountain, **the rocks shifting and sliding** beneath our boots.
8. We strolled through the park. The autumn leaves crunched under our shoes.
    » We strolled through the park, **the autumn leaves crunching** under our shoes.
9. The singer performed a powerful ballad. Her voice resonated through the concert hall.
    » The singer performed a powerful ballad, **her voice resonating** through the concert hall.

13.3A Combine these sentences by transforming one of them into a nominative absolute.

1. The exam was completed. The students were allowed to leave the classroom.
   » The exam completed, the students were allowed to leave the classroom.
   » With the exam completed, the students were allowed to leave the classroom.
2. The project was finished. The team celebrated with a well-deserved break.
   » The project finished, the team celebrated with a well-deserved break.
   » With the project finished, the team celebrated with a well-deserved break.
3. The issue was resolved. The customer was pleased with the company's service.
   » The issue resolved, the customer was pleased with the company's service.
   » With the issue resolved, the customer was pleased with the company's service.
4. The meeting was adjourned. The attendees filed out of the conference room.
   » The meeting adjourned, the attendees filed out of the conference room.
   » With the meeting adjourned, the attendees filed out of the conference room.
5. The speech was concluded. The audience gave the speaker a standing ovation.
   » The speech concluded, the audience gave the speaker a standing ovation.

6. The tourists were robbed. Their wallets were stolen in the crowded market.
    » The tourists were robbed, their wallets stolen in the crowded market.
7. The chef was frustrated. His dish was ruined by a mistake in the recipe.
    » The chef was frustrated, his dish ruined by a mistake in the recipe.
8. The recipe was laid out before her. She began mixing the ingredients to bake a delicious cake.
    » The recipe laid out before her, she began mixing the ingredients to bake a delicious cake.
    » With the recipe laid out before her, she began mixing the ingredients to bake a delicious cake.

Chapter 14

14.1A Sentence Combining

1. Hiking through the forest in the autumn, **we saw a deer**, an enormous male whitetail, ready for the winter in his thick, grey coat, completely unafraid of our presence, his enormous antlers a sign of his strength.
2. As the crowd watched, **the match began**, an arm wrestling competition held once a year, giving the winner the title of "strongest man in Latchford," Ontario's smallest town, population 387.
3. Having finally escaped the party, a high school reunion which they had not really enjoyed, the loud music making it impossible to communicate, **they drove and they talked**.
4. Lost in a new city, having given up waiting for her friend, **she walked in the rain**, a drizzle which had been falling all day, searching for a taxi.
5. Barely able to keep his eyes open, **he drank a cup of coffee**, black, the first of many that day, a day that would be filled with interminable meetings.
6. **He stepped away from the computer**, a sleek machine that was both a blessing and the bane of his existence, slamming it shut, dropping his glasses on top of it, his eyes weary of searching through infinite files for the missing data needed by his boss, a ruthless perfectionist who drove his employees to the breaking point, indifferent to their family lives, demanding total dedication to the job.

Printed in Dunstable, United Kingdom

79594286R00138